The
HERITAGE BOOK
2003

The HERITAGE BOOK *2003*

Edna McCann

HarperCollins*Publishers*Ltd

The Heritage Book 2003
Copyright © 2002 by Edna McCann.
All rights reserved. No part of this book
may be used or reproduced in any manner whatsoever without prior written
permission except in the case of brief
quotations embodied in reviews.
For information address
HarperCollins Publishers Ltd.,
55 Avenue Road, Suite 2900,
Toronto, Ontario, Canada M5R 3L2

www.harpercanada.com

HarperCollins books may be purchased
for educational, business, or sales promo-
tional use. For information please write:
Special Markets Department,
HarperCollins Canada,
55 Avenue Road, Suite 2900,
Toronto, Ontario, Canada M5R 3L2

First edition

Canadian Cataloguing in Publication Data

McCann, Edna
The heritage book

Annual.
1st ed. (1977)–
Issues for 2000– published
by HarperCollins.
ISSN 0711-4737
ISBN 0-00-200640-5 (2003 edition)

1. Anecdotes. 2. Maxims, English.
I. Title.

PN6331.M32   242'.2   C82-030470-0

WEB 9 8 7 6 5 4 3 2 1

Printed and bound in Canada
Set in New Caledonia

The author gratefully acknowledges the
following sources: "Snow Tracks" by
Georgia B. Adams. "In Love With
Spring" Georgia B. Adams. "Search for
Spring" by Ann Schneider. Reprinted
courtesy of the author. "My Grandma's
Garden" by Edna Jacques. Copyright ©
in Canada by Thomas Allen & Son.
Reprinted by permission of the pub-
lisher. "Enduring Things" by Mary E.
Linton. Reprinted courtesy of the
author. "The Fourth of July" Virginia K.
Oliver. "My Friend" from *Something
Beautiful* by Garnett Ann Schultz. Copy-
right © by the author. Reprinted by per-
mission of the author. "As September
Leaves" Elsie Grant. "Falling Leaves" by
William Arnette Wofford. "Snow Picture" by Nancy Byrd Turner.

Introduction

From the time that the first plane hit the World Trade Centre on the morning of September 11, 2001, our world changed irrevocably. The tragedy of that day, when people died in heartbreaking numbers, will ever be remembered, like Pearl Harbour, as a day that will live in infamy.

How does any good come from such devastation? How do we make our lives better after such horror?

For me, this time after September 11 has been a period of learning. On the day of the tragedy, our family members and a multitude of friends contacted one another just to say "I love you," "I miss you," or "I may never have told you how much you mean to me." This happened in families all across North America and most probably in countries around the world, as if we suddenly realized how precious and fleeting this life could be. I now take every opportunity to let my family know how important they are to me.

Watching the heroic efforts of police and firefighters in New York, Washington and Pennsylvania gave me a much greater appreciation for these brave men and women and the incredibly difficult job that is theirs. I will never take them for granted again.

When the order was issued to ground all planes,

many of them set down in Newfoundland. The thousands of stranded passengers were shown the hospitality so typical of those who live in Canada's easternmost province. They were fed, given places to shower, sleep or change their clothes. Television monitors were set up so that the stranded passengers could follow the terrible events. They were invited to stay in local schools, churches and homes. While the passengers and airline crews marvelled at the kindness shown to them, one of the Newfoundlanders expressed it well. "This generosity is not unusual. This is how we are." This sense of neighbourly kindness is something for us all to hold on to.

While we can never change the tragic events, I hope that we have learned that each of our days is a precious gift that we need to enjoy to the full.

"Life is short . . . do what makes you happy."

January

Wednesday January 1

On the first day of a wonderful new year, I decided against making New Year's resolutions. Instead, I have taken five simple sentence beginnings and completed them in ways that I hope will encourage me to think carefully about my life and how I wish to live the days in the year to come.

"I'm excited about" . . . being alive, having a book to write, a responsibility to fulfill and a goal to work toward.

"I'm grateful for" . . . good health, wonderful family, friends, country.

"I'm interested in" . . . the people I will meet this year, the miracles of nature, finding ways that will let me make this world a better place.

"I'm committed to" . . . a life of integrity, honesty, fair play, faith that sustains me, my church and my Lord.

"I'm confident of" . . . the wisdom of looking for the best in every person, the value of enthusiasm and the continued triumph of right over wrong.

Thursday January 2

If one cannot enjoy reading a book over and over again, there is no use reading it at all.

Oscar Wilde

This sentiment is one that I share completely. Although I read new books regularly, I have many favourites whose pages are becoming worn from use as I reread them time and again. One of these is *The Diary of Anne Frank*. Written by a young Jewish girl who, with her family, was forced to flee her home in Amsterdam and go into hiding from the Nazis, the diary offers a wise and most moving commentary on war and its impact on all of humankind. Her extraordinary insights give us a glimpse of a young woman whose promise was so tragically cut short.

I had occasion to reread and discuss this treasure recently, because my granddaughter Jenny, who has been studying World War II in her high school history class, was assigned the book as extra reading.

"You know, Gram, teachers and history books can tell me about the war, but Anne Frank's diary brought it to life. As I read this book I became her and all her feelings became mine. I have never read a book that moved me the way this one did."

I'm sure that this is one of the books that Jenny will reread through her life as well.

WINTER SHADOWS

Friday January 3

Don't believe the world owes you a living; the world owes you nothing. It was here first.

R. J. Burdette

Saturday January 4

The longer I live, the more I am convinced that the one thing worth living for and dying for is the privilege of making someone more happy and more useful. No man who ever does anything to lift his fellows ever makes a sacrifice.

Booker T. Washington

Sunday January 5

God who touchest earth with beauty
Make my heart anew;
With thy Spirit re-create me,
Pure, and strong and true.

Like thy springs and running waters,
Make me crystal pure;
Like thy rocks of towering grandeur,
Make me strong and sure.

Mary S. Edgar

Monday January 6

Epiphany

Today is the celebration of Epiphany. In the Western Church, it is the day to commemorate the coming of the Three Wise Men, who were led by the Star of Bethlehem to the birthplace of the infant Jesus.

As with gladness men of old
Did the guiding star behold,
As with joy they hailed its light,
Leading onward, beaming bright;
So, most gracious Lord, may we
Evermore be led to Thee.

William Chatterton Dix

Tuesday January 7

On a miserably cold, nasty day such as this, I was delighted to spend several hours in front of the fireplace savouring my memories of the holiday just past. Often we are so busy and caught up in the details of these special times that we may not enjoy them as much as we should.

Sometimes it takes a restful day and some time alone to really appreciate the happy days just past.

Wednesday January 8

The experience of the world has proved that the idle man, though he be living in luxury, is never the happy man, but on the contrary, is lost in a kind of sad confusion, as he seeks in vain for the rewards which he thought he found. The

happy man is the one who makes his work, whatever it is, the essence of his life, and cannot be
separated from it.

Anonymous

Thursday January 9

I thank the unknown author for these lines for
today.

Three Gates

If I am tempted to reveal
A tale someone to me has told
About another, let it pass,
Before I speak, three gates of gold.

Three narrow gates: First, is it true?
Then, is it needful? In my mind
Give truthful answer, and the next
Is last and narrowest, is it kind?

And if to reach my lips at last,
It passes through these gateways, three,
Then I may tell the tale, nor fear
What the result of speech may be.

Friday January 10

When the winter is cold and dreary, I often
turn to "comfort foods" to brighten my day.
Soup is one of my favourites and this recipe is
especially nice because it is simple but delicious.

Super Sweet Potato & Pear Soup

1 tbsp. butter
1 small onion, chopped
1/4 cup chopped carrot
1/4 cup chopped celery
3 medium sweet potatoes, peeled and diced
2 pears, peeled and diced
1/2 tsp. dried thyme
1 tsp. paprika
5 cups chicken broth (either home-made or
canned / low salt)
1/3 cup whipping cream
2 tsp. maple syrup (or to taste)
2 tsp. lime juice (or to taste)

In a large pot melt the butter on medium heat. Add onion, carrot and celery and sauté for 2 minutes. Add the sweet potatoes, pears and thyme and sauté for 2 minutes. Add paprika and chicken broth. Bring mixture to a boil. Simmer for 15 minutes or until the sweet potatoes are soft.

Purée mixture in a blender or food processor until smooth. Return to pot.

Add cream. Simmer for 5 minutes. Season with salt and pepper and add maple syrup and lime juice to taste.

Serves 6.

Saturday January 11

Some years ago, some friends of ours decided to sell their home and move to a larger place to accommodate their growing family. For several months the real estate company ran ads—all of which sounded something like this: "Cozy three bedroom two storey with fireplace, single car garage, 1 1/2 baths. Convenient to schools, shopping and the local golf course." There was very little interest until Mildred took a hand in advertising the home on her own.

Her ad read, "We'll surely miss our home. As much as we loved living here, three bedrooms are not enough for us now and we need to move. If you would enjoy sitting by the fire and watching the deer that occasionally wander onto our lawn from the woods out back, or listening for robins in spring; if you enjoy that country feeling but like being close to the conveniences of the city, you might want to buy our home. We really hope so because we don't want our home to be empty and alone at Thanksgiving."

The house sold two days after this ad ran.

Sunday January 12

O come, let us sing to the Lord; let us make a joyful noise to the rock of our salvation.

Let us come into his presence with thanksgiving; let us make a joyful noise to him with songs of praise.

For the Lord is a great God, and a great King above all gods.

Psalm 95:1–3

Monday January 13

My good friend Emily passed on these wise thoughts for those of us who are growing older.

1. I will not try to act nor dress nor talk so as to make people think I am younger than I am.
2. I will not pretend to be young, nor be angry when called old, nor be ashamed of my age.
3. I will not complain of being old.
4. I will not continually remind people of my old age to secure their sympathy, or to hear them say I am not so old after all or do not seem so.
5. I will not form the habit of indulging in reminiscences.
6. I will be particularly careful not to repeat the same anecdotes over and over.
7. I will not complain about the present and claim the past was better.
8. If I am deaf, weak-eyed or otherwise afflicted, I will not advertise my infirmities, but avoid obtruding them on the notice of others as much as possible.
9. I will not talk of myself, my work, my

achievements, even of my mistakes any more than necessary.

10. I will speak cheerfully or keep still.
11. I will never indulge in cynicism, never sneer at youth, and will always try to appreciate what younger folks do.
12. I shall concede my life's triumph to be to grow triumphantly, victoriously old.
13. In a word, I shall try to adjust myself to old age, as well as to all other facts of life.

Tuesday January 14

If we want to change our lives we must first change our attitudes. Happiness is not created by what happens to us but by our attitude toward each happening.

Wednesday January 15

Today is the birthday of Dr. Martin Luther King, Jr., the African American statesman and winner of the Nobel Peace Prize. The late Dr. King was a strong proponent of the strategy of non-violent civil disobedience in the struggle for black equality in the United States.

The following thoughts give us a good idea of Dr. King's eloquence.

Man was born into barbarism, when killing his fellow man was a normal condition of existence. He became endowed with a conscience. And he has now reached the day when violence toward another human being must be as abhorrent as eating another's flesh.

Darkness cannot drive out darkness; only light can do that. Hate cannot drive out hate; only love can do that. Hate multiplies hate, violence multiplies violence, and toughness multiplies toughness in a descending spiral of destruction. . . . The chain reaction of evil—hate begetting hate, wars producing more wars—must be broken, or we shall be plunged into the dark abyss of annihilation.

Power at its best is love implementing the demands of justice. Justice at its best is love correcting everything that stands against love.

Thursday January 16

If we can say with Seneca, "This life is only a prelude to eternity," then we need not worry so much over the fittings and furnishings of the anteroom; and more than that, it will give dignity and purpose to the fleeting days to know they are linked with the eternal things as prelude and preparation.

M. J. Savage

Friday January 17

I hope you enjoy these lines from Annie Johnson Flint as much as I do.

God hath not promised skies always blue,
Flower-strewn pathways all our lives through;
God hath not promised sun without rain,
Joy without sorrow, peace without pain.
But God hath promised strength for the day,
Rest for the labourer, light on the way,
Grace for the trials, help from above,
Unfailing sympathy, undying love.

Saturday January 18

The average person is a liberal in matters in his favour, a moderate about things that don't particularly affect him and a conservative when it comes to something that would benefit others at his expense.

Thomas La Mance

Sunday January 19

It is a good thing to give thanks unto the Lord, and to sing praises unto thy name, O most High: To shew forth thy loving kindness in the morning, and thy faithfulness every night,

Upon an instrument of ten strings, and upon the psaltery; upon the harp with a solemn sound.

For thou, Lord, hast made me glad through thy work: I will triumph in the works of thy hands.

O Lord, how great are thy works! and thy thoughts are very deep.

Psalm 92:1–5

Monday January 20

These lines have been attributed to Mother Teresa. They are wise words to live by.

If you are kind, people may accuse you of
　selfish motives;
Be kind anyway.
What you spend years building, someone
　could destroy overnight;
Build anyway.
If you find serenity and happiness, others
　may be jealous;
Be happy anyway.
The good you do today, people will often
　forget tomorrow;
Do good anyway.
Give the world the best you have, and it may
　never be enough;
Give the world the best you have anyway.

Tuesday January 21

Our neighbours have five teenage sons—all with the enormous appetites for which teenage boys are well known.

Pat, their mother, explained this to me over tea one day.

"You know, Edna, keeping enough food in the house to feed these kids is a never-ending chore. Many times I've tried to do extra baking to put into our freezer. I think I have enough for several weeks ahead only to find, when I go to look for something, that one of the boys has been there first and a whole tin (or tins) of cookies have already been eaten.

This totally frustrated me until this past Christmas. I did an enormous amount of baking—cookies, tarts, muffins, cupcakes, dozens of everything! This time, though, as I packed them into the storage containers I had a brilliant idea. I placed the tins into the freezer, each one carefully labelled as 'sliced zucchini' or 'squash casserole' or 'brussels sprouts.'

When I needed any of my baked goods they were all there, right where I left them! As long as the boys don't figure it out, this could be one of my best plans."

Wednesday January 22

Never fear shadows. They simply mean that there is a light shining nearby.

Thursday January 23

When I see an honoured friend again after years of separation, it is like resuming the words of an old conversation which has been halted by time. As one gets older, friendship becomes more precious to us, for it affirms the contours of our existence. It is a reservoir of shared experience, of having lived through many things in our brief and mutual moment on earth.

W. Morris

Friday January 24

With the nasty weather of today, I didn't leave the house at all. As I looked outside to see the snow falling heavily and the wind arranging the snow in enormous drifts, I was reminded of an anecdote that my grandson Marshall told me some years ago.

The owner of a bakery was closing shop on a stormy winter's night when a man came in and asked for two sweet rolls. The baker was amazed that anyone would come out in such weather for just two sweet rolls.

"Are you married?" the baker asked.

"Of course," replied the gentleman. "Do you think my mother would send me out on a night like this?"

Saturday January 25

Today is the birthday of Robbie Burns, the celebrated Scottish poet. My mother was proud of her Scottish ancestry, and she instilled in us that same sense of pride. I do confess, however, that none of us ever became fond of haggis, the "treat" so often served on this day.

Life is but a day at most,
Sprung from night—in darkness lost:
Hope not sunshine ev'ry hour,
Fear not clouds will always lour.

Sunday January 26

Blessed are you when people revile you and persecute you and utter all kinds of evil against you falsely on my account. Rejoice and be glad, for your reward is great in heaven.

Mathew 5:11–12

Monday January 27

After all allowances are made for the necessity of having a few supermen in our midst—explorers, conquerors, great inventors, great presidents, heroes who change the course of history—the happiest man is still the man of the middle class who has earned a slight means of economic independence, who has done a little, but just a little, for mankind, and who is slightly distinguished in his community, but not too distinguished.

Lin Yutang

Tuesday January 28

There are a number of very special people in the Terry Fox Hall of Fame, perhaps none more so than Ivy Granstrom, who was inducted as an athlete in 2001—at the age of 90.

Blind her whole life, Ivy came to running rather late in the game. At age 64 she was hit by a car, and doctors told her that she would be confined to a wheelchair. Undaunted, she learned to walk again and then to run, first short distances and then distances up to 10,000 metres. She holds 25 world records for Master athletes who are over 60 years of age.

In her acceptance speech, she said, "Running is more than something I do. It is a way of life for me. My great privilege over the years has been meeting and touching people around the world, especially the children, who come to watch me run. Living with a disability does not mean living with a lack of possibility. I strive each day to overcome negative influences and thoughts—to go ahead in the world with a positive attitude and work hard toward my goals. The only inability I know is the inability to say 'I can't.'

Terry Fox sparked the imagination of our country and the world. His legacy is immense, and I only hope my experience might serve, in some small way, as another reminder that so much in life is possible."

Wednesday January 29

The best preparation for work is not thinking about work, talking about work or studying for work. It is work.

William Weld

Thursday January 30

> The world is a great mirror.
> It reflects back to you what you are.
> If you are loving, if you are friendly and help-
> ful, the world will prove loving and friendly
> and helpful to you.
> The world is what you are.
>
> *Thomas Dreier*

Friday January 31

I spent an hour at the dentist's office today, and I surprise myself by saying that I enjoyed it very much. As one who has always feared the dentist, I now find my visits to be pleasant and far less worrisome than previously.

In early times, the most common treatment of diseased teeth was extraction. The procedure was done by one of three horrific methods. One was to loosen the tooth by applying caustics. Another was to insert a dry peppercorn into the cavity. The peppercorn would soon swell so large that it would break the tooth into pieces. Most commonly, the patient lay with his head between the doctor's knees while dental tongs rocked the tooth until it came out.

Although I was never subjected to this horrify-ing treatment, I had heard about it from older relatives and their stories struck fear into my young heart, making each visit for me a terrifying experience. Thank goodness for the advances in modern dentistry.

February

Saturday February 1

I enjoyed the "Ten Commandments For Happiness" that my friend Mildred passed along to me.

(1) Thou shalt cultivate a sense of humour, and remember that much gloom has been created by those who take life too seriously.

(2) Thou shalt not despise thy body, but develop it for strength and beauty. Eat wholesome food, exercise regularly and take plenty of sleep.

(3) Thou shalt have a dominating, worth-while purpose in thy life, and allow nothing to turn thee from its fulfillment.

(4) Thou shalt look upon thy job as the most important thing in the world, and strive ever to do it perfectly.

(5) Thou shalt be thyself. Never seek to imitate another.

(6) Thou shalt live within thy means, thy own desires, thy neighbour's appearances and high-pressure salesmen notwithstanding.

(7) Thou shalt not worry; neither shalt thou be nervous or fearful of the future, for worry is the death of happiness.

(8) Thou shalt do well to be acquainted with Nature, for many have thereby discovered beauty, melody and fragrance in life.

(9) Thou shalt take care never to seek for happiness, for it is one thing which seeking thou canst not find.

(10) Thou shalt, above all, strive ever to contribute to the happiness of others, for in so doing, thou shalt discover happiness in thine own mind.

Anonymous

Sunday February 2

They that wait upon the Lord shall renew their strength; they shall mount up with wings as eagles; they shall run, and not be weary; and they shall walk, and not faint.

Isaiah 40:31

Monday February 3

Yesterday was Groundhog Day, that day when, according to superstition, the woodchuck becomes a weather prognosticator. In our area, the groundhog was able to see his shadow, meaning that our winter weather is to continue for six weeks more. Although it is merely a superstition, the groundhog has a rather surprisingly high percentage of accuracy. I sincerely hope that this year he has made an error in his forecast. I, for one, am ready for an early spring!

Tuesday February 4

Our family members have long been fans of trivia. I think it began with my father who, at the dinner table, would impart some particular piece of information—the stranger the better. My husband, George, had an interest in things unusual as well, so our evening meals became almost a competition to see who could come up with the most interesting or ridiculous bits of knowledge. Games such as "Trivial Pursuit" along with television programs "Jeopardy" and "Who Wants to Be a Millionaire" have all kept our trivia interest at a high level.

My grandson Marshall came up with the following bits of information. I thought you might have some fun dazzling your friends or neighbours with these gems.

More than 45,000 pieces of plastic debris float on every square mile of ocean.

The average person blinks 25 times per minute, which is about 13,140,000 blinks per year.

A small or imperfect ear of corn is called a nubbin.

Beetles taste like apples, wasps like pine nuts, and white worms like dried pork rinds. (I wonder who decided to try eating them?)

A cubic mile of ordinary fog contains less than a gallon of water.

Or my favourite—ten books on a shelf can be arranged in 3,628,800 different ways.

Wednesday February 5

As our cold snap continues, I laughed at this anecdote from Richard Ketchum.

One morning we ran into a neighbour at the store and she asked brightly, "What was it at your house?"

"Fourteen below," we replied.

Her face fell! "We had minus twelve," she said, and you could see that her day was ruined.

Thursday February 6

Instead of allowing yourself to be unhappy, just let your love grow as God wants it to grow. Seek goodness in others. Love more persons more. Love them more impersonally, more unselfishly, without thought of return. The return, never fear, will take care of itself.

Henry Drummond

Friday February 7

It's the giving and doing for someone else
On that, all life's splendour depends.
And the joys of this life, when you sum them
all up,
Are found in the making of friends.

Saturday February 8

After spending several hours in the hockey arena watching my great-grandson Michael's hockey game, I am happy to get home to a good dinner. Happily, Marg had made a stew early this morning so it was perfect for our evening meal.

Chuckwagon Stew

2 lbs. beef chuck, cut in 1 1/2" cubes
4 cups water *
1 medium onion, sliced
1 tsp. salt
1 tsp. sugar
1/2 tsp. pepper
1 tsp. Worcestershire sauce
1 tbsp. lemon juice
1/2 cup chopped celery
6 carrots, quartered
1/2 lb. small white onions
3 potatoes, quartered
1 16 oz. can tomatoes
4 tbsp. flour
1/2 cup cold water

Trim excess fat from the beef; heat the fat in a Dutch oven. Brown the meat slowly on all sides

* Drain the canned tomatoes and use the juice as part of the 4 cups of water.

in the hot fat. Add water, sliced onions and seasonings. Cover and simmer (do not boil) for 2 hours, stirring occasionally to keep from sticking. Add vegetables (except tomatoes) and cook covered for 20 minutes. Add tomatoes and cook 15 minutes longer or until meat and vegetables are tender. Skim the fat from the stew.

To thicken the liquid, pour 4 tbsp. of flour into a small bowl; slowly stir in 1/2 cup of cold water—the mixture must be smooth, no lumps. Stir into the stew; cook, stirring constantly, until thickened. Cook 5 minutes more.

Makes 6–8 servings.

This is delicious served with hot biscuits and thick wedges of cheddar cheese.

Sunday February 9

> What a friend we have in Jesus,
> All our sins and griefs to bear!
> What a privilege to carry
> Everything to God in prayer.
> O what peace we often forfeit,
> O what needless pain we bear,
> All because we do not carry
> Everything to God in prayer.
>
> *Joseph Scriven*

Monday February 10

Memory is a capricious and arbitrary creature.

You can never tell what pebble she will pick up from the shore of life to keep among her treasures, or what inconspicuous flower of the field she will preserve as the symbol of thoughts that do often "lie too deep for tears."

And yet I do not doubt that the most important things are always the best remembered.

Henry Van Dyke

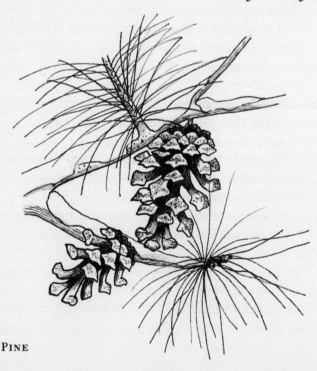

PINE

Tuesday February 11

My friend Marcia recently spent several weeks in Paris, France. As her trip was planned many months in advance, she decided to take a course in conversational French, hoping that, if nothing else, she would be able to order her meals in restaurants in the native language. When I asked her about her experiences, her response was very amusing.

"Edna, I really thought that I had a pretty good grasp of the French language. I studied for months. . . . I listened to tapes in my car, and I repeated every phrase so carefully. On our first evening out my friend and I went to a charming little restaurant on the left bank, and I decided to dazzle everyone with my newly acquired skill. I greeted the maître d' with my most confident 'Bonsoir, monsieur.' Apparently I was not as fluent as I had assumed because he replied immediately, 'Ah, you are American visitors in France. Fortunately, madame, we also have ze menu in English.' I was keenly disappointed."

Her experience brought to mind these words from other American visitors in France.

In Paris they simply stared when I spoke to them in French; I never did succeed in making those idiots understand their own language.

Mark Twain

An American who speaks French can only be understood by other Americans who have also just arrived in Paris.

Fred Allen

Wednesday February 12
Life is mostly froth and bubble;
Two things stand like stone:
Kindness in another's trouble,
Courage in our own.

Thursday February 13
Let us be grateful to people who make us happy. They are the charming gardeners who make our souls blossom.

Marcel Proust

Friday February 14

St. Valentine's Day
My husband, George, always made this day a very special one. Even as we struggled to make ends meet on a minister's salary, George would find a way to do something that showed how much he loved and cared for me and our three daughters.

After George's passing, other members of my family wanted to keep Valentine's Day a special one for me. Each year someone (and I never know who it is) sends me a wonderful gift. One year it may be a floral bouquet, another, a gift certificate to a nearby restaurant or perhaps a box of my favourite chocolates. The card always reads, "From your secret Valentine."

Children have never been very good at listening to their elders, but they have never failed to imitate them.

James Baldwin

Saturday February 15

After the snow of last evening, these lines from Georgia B. Adams came to mind.

Snow Tracks

I love to be the first to make
Tracks on the driven snow,
Bent on a bit of adventuring
And laughing as I go.

There with snow still falling
In a wonderland of white,
I stake my claim as first to see
This peaceful, awesome sight.

All man-made paths are drifted shut,
The world is mine to roam;
What fun to venture forth in snow
A little way from home.

My steps like giant-tracks appear,
A backward look reveals;
I find myself believing that
A giant stalks my heels.

I love to be the first to take
Steps in the trackless snow,
Adventuring with baited breath
And laughing as I go!

Sunday February 16

Trust in the Lord with all thine heart; and lean not unto thine own understanding. In all thy ways acknowledge him, and he shall direct thy paths.

Proverbs 3:5–6

Monday February 17

My friend Jake Frampton owns a small used bookstore and, because of his voracious reading of books of all kinds, he always has some interesting, little-known stories to tell. Today was no exception.

William Cowper, the well-known English poet, was once contemplating suicide. Leaving his London apartment, he hailed a horse-drawn hansom cab and instructed the driver to take him to the banks of the Thames River. There he intended to drown himself. There was a thick fog that evening, and the driver became lost. After nearly an hour's drive, Cowper abandoned the cab, determined to walk to the river. To his surprise and amazement, he found himself in front of his own door. The driver had somehow driven in a circle. Seeing the irony in the situation, Cowper returned to his room and wrote these immortal lines:

God works in a mysterious way
His wonders to perform,
He plants His footsteps in the sea
And rides upon the storm.

Tuesday February 18

Something to keep in mind at this time of year is the health risk in shovelling snow. According to experts, a combination of cold air and upper-body strain makes shovelling snow one of the greatest challenges to the heart.

Research studies have shown that after only two minutes of shovelling heavy, wet snow, subjects' heart rates exceeded the upper limit for exercise training (85 per cent of maximum heart rate). Heart rate and blood pressure also continued to rise during the ten minute shovelling session being monitored.

With these thoughts in mind, experts suggest that if you have not been exercising regularly, or if you are at risk for coronary heart disease due to high blood pressure, or high cholesterol, or if you are a heavy smoker, you should check with your doctor before you decide to shovel off your walkway or driveway. Be "snow safe," not sorry.

Wednesday February 19

The first time I read an excellent book, it is to me as if I had gained a new friend. When I read over a book I have perused before, it resembles a meeting with an old one.

Oliver Goldsmith

Thursday February 20

My daughter Julia is a cat fancier and one of those people who believes that cats are the most intelligent of all pets. A good friend of mine sent me a "Cat Diary," and I dedicate this to Julia.

Day 752—My captors continue to taunt me with bizarre little dangling objects. They dine lavishly on fresh meat, while I am forced to eat dry cereal. The only thing that keeps me going is the hope of escape, and the mild satisfaction that I get from shredding the occasional piece of furniture. Tomorrow I may eat another houseplant and cough it up on the carpeting.

Day 762—Slept all day so that I could annoy my captors with sleep-depriving, incessant pleas for food at ungodly hours of the night.

Day 765—Decapitated a mouse and brought them the headless body in an attempt to make them aware of what I am capable of, and to try to strike fear into their hearts. They only cooed about what a good little cat I was . . . hmmm . . . not working according to plan.

Day 774—I am convinced the other captives are flunkies and may be snitches. The dog is routinely released and seems more than happy to return. He is obviously a half-wit. The bird, on the other hand, has got to be an informant. He has mastered their frightful tongue (something akin to mole speak) and speaks with them regularly. I am certain he reports my every move. Due to his current placement in the metal room, his safety is assured.

But I can wait . . . it is only a matter of time.

Friday February 21

Real generosity is doing something nice for someone who will never find it out.

Saturday February 22

Treasure the love you receive above all. It will survive long after your gold and good health have vanished.

O. Mandino

Sunday February 23

Rest of the weary,
Joy of the sad,
Hope of the dreary,
Light of the glad,

Home of the stranger,
Strength to the end,
Refuge from danger
Saviour and friend.

Rev. J. S. B. Monsell

Monday February 24

It is a good idea to be ambitious, to want to be good at what you do, to have goals; but it is a terrible mistake to let drive and ambition get in the way of treating people with kindness and decency. The point is not that they will then be nice to you. It is that you will feel better about yourself.

Robert Solow

Tuesday February 25

Andy Rooney said it well: it's paradoxical that the idea of living a long life appeals to everyone, but the idea of getting old doesn't appeal to anyone.

Wednesday February 26

Fundraising for church repairs was always part of a minister's job that George found onerous. My son-in-law John, also a minister, told me this story that I'm sure would have made George laugh.

"Because the church was old and in a poor

state of repair, the minister was trying to raise funds for a new church.

One Sunday, after a sermon, the minister called on parishioners for pledges. One member rose and declared, 'I pledge $50.00.' Just at that moment a piece of plaster fell from the ceiling onto his head. Stunned, the man mumbled, 'All right then, $500.00.'

'O, Lord' the minister prayed, 'Please hit him again.' "

Thursday February 27

If a man walks in the woods for the love of them, for half of each day, he is in danger of being regarded as a loafer. But if he spends his day as a speculator, shearing off those woods and making the earth bald before her time, he is esteemed an industrious and enterprising citizen.

Henry David Thoreau

Friday February 28

My good friend Mildred lost her husband several months ago. She has found that one of the things she misses most is company at mealtime. I, too, found this to be a very difficult time, particularly at the dinner hour, as George and I would often review the day that had just passed.

As I explained to Mildred, although I had

never watched much television, I found that I came to enjoy its company at supper. Just hearing another voice provided comfort for me. Mildred has decided she will give this a try.

March

Saturday March 1

The Simple Things

Give me the simple things close to my home,
   The things that are familiar, old and dear,
I do not have to wander far, or roam
   The Seven Seas—when I have splendor
   here.

Give me a crackling flame upon the grate
   And warm smell of bread upon the fire.
I do not have to ride abroad in state
   To find the very core of heart's desire.

Sunday March 2

O Lord, our heavenly Father, almighty and
everlasting God, who hast safely brought us
to the beginning of this day: Defend us in the
same with thy mighty power; and grant that this
day we fall into no sin, neither run into any kind
of danger; but that we, being ordered by thy gov-
ernance, may do always what is righteous in thy
sight; through Jesus Christ our Lord. Amen.

A Collect for Grace
The Book of Common Prayer

Monday March 3

For the past several years, some of the most popular children's books have been those of the *Harry Potter* series, written by British author J. K. Rowling.

Harry, a 12-year-old boy living with his aunt and uncle, makes an amazing discovery—he is a wizard. In the first book, *Harry Potter and the Philosopher's Stone,* Harry spends his first year at the Hogwarts School of Witchcraft and Wizardry. Here, he learns to cast spells and to play Quidditch, a popular sport in the wizardly world.

Ms. Rowling provides a spectacular cast of characters and a splendid plot full of mystery and magic, appealing to young and old alike. Several of my great-grandchildren became enthralled with these books and I, when reading to the children, became equally enthusiastic about these entertaining and thrilling books. I found it especially exciting to see how the children's imaginations were stimulated. So often television shows and computer games leave children little room for creative development. Ms. Rowlings' books have opened the window of imaginative opportunity and drawn readers into a world of magic and wonder. What author could ever ask for more?

Tuesday March 4

We may not be responsible for all the things that happen to us, but we are responsible for the way we behave when they do happen.

Wednesday March 5

Ash Wednesday

Then he will answer them, "Truly I tell you, just as you did not do it to one of the least of these, you did not do it to me."

Mathew 25:45

Thursday March 6

All of us want to be good Samaritans when a family member or friend is in the hospital, but our visits could turn out to be "bad medicine" for seriously ill patients. These suggestions, from hospital staff, make excellent sense to all.

Remember to limit the time that you stay. People who have been ill are often weak and may tire easily. Fifteen minutes is the time suggested by most physicians, ten minutes if the patient has other company.

If a patient wants to talk about his or her illness, be a good listener, but don't initiate this conversation. Talking of times you have enjoyed together or bringing news of friends often gives a patient a lift. In an effort to be cheerful, many people raise their voices. A quiet voice is much more sooth-ing—don't yell. Thoughtful gifts might include puzzles, decks of cards or magazines.

If a doctor believes that many visitors, phone calls et cetera will help morale, he or she will tell the patient's family. The best rule of thumb to follow would seem to be: never visit anyone who is sick unless you are a close relative or friend.

Good advice for us all.

Friday March 7

I thank the unknown author for these lines for today.

I got a dozen roses
From a friend the other day,
But I only have one left,
For I gave them all away.

I gave one to my sister
Who to me is very dear,
In hopes that it will bring to her
A little floral cheer.

MARCH

I took one to a friend
Who's not feeling very well,
The flower or the visit
Which helped more . . . I could not tell.

One went to a friend
I haven't known for very long:
She struggles . . . so in some small way
I hope this helps her carry on.

The rest went to the ones
Who've helped me in so many ways;
They have been a cheerful presence
On my very dreary days.

The roses were so pretty
I just could not keep them all,
Except one single bud standing
Beautiful and tall.

My friend gave me the flowers
To help brighten up my day,
But the biggest joy that I received
Was in giving them away.

Saturday March 8

The pleasantest things in the world are pleasant thoughts, and the great art of life is to have as many of them as possible.

Sunday March 9

Almighty God, your son fasted forty days in the wilderness and was tempted but did not sin. Give us grace to discipline ourselves in submission to your spirit, that as you know our weakness, so may we know your power to save; through Jesus Christ our Lord, who is alive and reigns with you and the Holy Spirit, one God now and forever. Amen.

Monday March 10

When you consider how hard it is to change yourself, it makes it much easier to understand what little chance you have of trying to change others.

Tuesday March 11

I grew up on Canada's east coast and my sister, Sarah, and her husband, Richard, still live in this beautiful area. Richard made me laugh today with this story. I can't vouch for its authenticity, but Richard swears that it is true.

This is an actual radio conversation of a U.S. naval ship with Canadian authorities off the coast of Newfoundland in October 1995.

Canadians: Please divert your course 15 degrees south to avoid a collision.

Americans: Recommend that you divert your course 15 degrees to the north to avoid a collision.

Canadians: Negative. You will have to divert your course 15 degrees to the south to avoid a collision.

Americans: This is the captain of a U.S. Navy ship. I say again, divert your course!

Canadians: No, I say again, you divert your course!

Americans: This is the aircraft carrier USS Lincoln, the second largest ship in the U.S. Atlantic fleet. We are accompanied by three destroyers, three cruisers and numerous support vessels. I DEMAND that you change your course 15 degrees north. I say again, that is one five degrees north, or counter measures will be taken to ensure the safety of this vessel.

Canadians: This is a lighthouse. Your call.

Wednesday March 12

Long ago, the Native Americans of the Great Plains survived the harsh winters by having grandparents and grandchildren sleep beside each other to keep from freezing to death. That is a good metaphor for what the generations do for each other. The old need our heat, and we need their light.

Mary Pipher

Thursday March 13

If faith can move mountains, imagine what hard work can do.

Friday March 14

Sometimes those of us with good vision see less than those who are blind. Read these lines from Helen Keller to see what I mean.

"I asked a friend who had just returned from a long walk in the woods what she had observed. 'Nothing in particular,' she replied.

"How is that possible, I asked myself. I, who cannot hear or see, find hundreds of things to interest me through mere touch. I feel the delicate symmetry of a leaf. I pass my hand lovingly about the rough shaggy bark of a pine. Occasionally, if I am very fortunate, I place my hand gently on a small tree and feel the happy quiver of a bird in full song."

Saturday March 15

Ours is a family of chocolate lovers, and dessert for us isn't really dessert unless it's made with chocolate. Chocolate mint pudding is one of our favourites. I hope you'll enjoy it too.

Chocolate Mint Pudding

1/2 cup sugar
2 tbsp. cornstarch
2 1/2 cups whole milk

yolks of four large eggs
1 tsp. vanilla extract
1/8 tsp. peppermint extract
1 cup semisweet chocolate chips
8 crème de menthe thins (such as Andes
  mints) coarsely chopped
Garnish: whipped cream, Andes mints, cut in
  triangles

Mix sugar and cornstarch in a medium bowl. Gradually whisk in milk and egg yolks until blended. Bring to a boil, stirring occasionally. Reduce heat to low and whisk 2 minutes or until thickened. Remove from heat. Stir in vanilla and peppermint extract.

Add chocolate chips; let stand 1 minute to melt. Whisk until blended. Let cool 10 minutes, then gently fold in chopped mints.

Spoon into glasses or a bowl. Cover the pudding surface to prevent a skin from forming. Refrigerate 2 to 3 hours or until the pudding is well chilled. To serve, garnish with whipped cream and mint triangles.

Serves 6.

Sunday March 16

Jesus said to them, "Follow me and I will make you fish for people." Immediately they left their nets and followed him.

Mathew 4:19–20

Monday March 17

On this St. Patrick's Day, I offer you a traditional Irish blessing.

> May you always have
> Walls for the winds
> A roof for the rain
> Tea beside the fire
> Laughter to cheer you
> Those you love near you
> And all your heart
> Might desire.

Tuesday March 18

I believe that these words from John Ruskin are fine words to live by.

Let every dawn of morning be to you a new beginning of life and every setting sun be to you as its close; then let every one of these short lives leave its sure record of some kindly thing done for others, some goodly strength or knowledge gained for yourself.

Wednesday March 19

One of the most difficult things for many of us to accept is that we are no longer young. In fact, we need a lot of courage to face what we have become: old. In talking with friends we have concluded that there is probably nothing more important than aging gracefully and hopefully, without complaining too much about our infirmities. A cartoon in the *New Yorker* magazine some years ago showed an elderly couple walking along a beach. The woman is speaking. "Harold, I know your problems are serious, they're just not very interesting."

My dear friend Emily, who has never been one to complain about anything, recently read these suggestions from Gordon Livingston, a psychiatrist in Columbia, Maryland.

"Stop complaining. Had you been from an earlier generation, you would have been dead for ten years.

"If you don't have an activity that makes you lose track of time, get one.

"If you visit a doctor more than 10 times a year and you don't have a terminal illness, get a new hobby.

"Although it is probably true that no good music has been written in the last few years, neither your children nor your grandchildren want to hear about it.

"If anyone wants to know what life was like when you were their age, they will ask.

"Courage is ageless. Relinquish dignity last."

Thursday March 20

Each morning upon rising and each evening before sleeping, give thanks to the life within you and for all life, for the good things the Creator has given you and others, and for the opportunity to grow a little more each day. Consider your thoughts and actions of the past and seek the courage and strength to be a better person. Seek for those things that will benefit everyone.

Lesson one of the Native Code of Ethics

Friday March 21

Today is the first day of spring, and I welcome this new season joyfully. Georgia B. Adams wrote a wonderful poem to celebrate this day.

In Love With Spring

I fell in love with spring today!
It happens every year,
For when I hear a robin's note,
His gladness and his cheer. . . .

And when I see the azaleas
In crimson beauty rise;
The brightly coloured tulip reaching
Toward the sunlit skies.

And when I scoop a handful of
The rich brown earth again,
And feel the very pulse of it,
It is right there and then

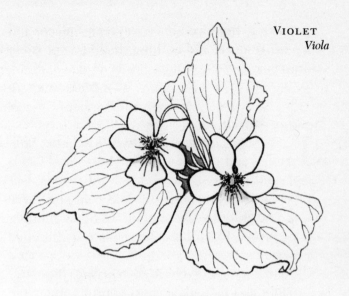

VIOLET
Viola

I fall a helpless victim to
The season's wealth of cheer,
I fall in love with spring anew. . . .
It happens every year!

Saturday March 22

The pathway to success is in serving human-ity. By no other means is it possible, and this truth is so plain and patent that even very simple folk can recognize it.

Elbert Hubbard

Sunday March 23

Verily I say unto you, If ye have faith as a grain of mustard seed, ye shall say unto this mountain, Remove hence to yonder place; and it shall remove; and nothing shall be impossible unto you.

Mathew 17:20

Monday March 24

Last Saturday my grandson Fred, his wife June, and their two boys, Mickey and Geoffrey, and I spent a lovely day in the woods near their farm. Although it was still cold and there was a fair bit of snow around, we hiked into the bush where Fred had a large store of chopped firewood. After the boys built a fire, we warmed the large crock of baked beans that June had brought and that, along with hot rolls and apple cider, made a delicious picnic lunch.

The peace and quiet of the forest was almost eerie. It seemed to be too early to find any signs of spring, and even the birds were silent.

It was a delightful way to spend an early spring day. As "un-spring-like" as the weather was, we could feel the promise of better things to come.

Spring . . . it is a natural resurrection, an experience of immortality.

Henry David Thoreau

Tuesday March 25

Wisdom is knowing what to do next; skill is knowing how to do it, and virtue is doing it.
David Starr Jordan

Wednesday March 26

Some years ago, Bruce was concerned about his son Marshall. As a young adult out on his own, Marshall was about to make some important career choices. Phone calls between them had grown tense because Bruce had some definite opinions about the decisions to be made.

Although Bruce originally planned to write Marshall a letter that detailed his concerns and included much advice, something made him change his mind. Instead he sat down and wrote a letter of encouragement detailing Marshall's strengths and gifts and the great confidence that Bruce had in his ability to make wise choices.

The letter was just the thing that Marshall needed. He made his decisions, and the realization that his father had enough confidence in him to trust those choices cemented a warm and loving relationship that endures to this day.

Thursday March 27

A man's life consists not of what he has, but what he is.

Friday March 28

Where others see but dawn coming over the hill, I see the soul of God shouting for joy.

William Blake

Saturday March 29

Spring! Ah, the sound of the word makes the heart dance and sing. Spring!

Sunday March 30

Jesus said, My sheep hear my voice. I know them and they follow me. I give them eternal life and they will never perish. No one will snatch them out of my hand.

John 10:27–28

Monday March 31

My daughter Julia is one of those people who seems to enjoy each and every day of her life. She has always been this way, even as a child, and I was remembering today the comment on her report card from an insightful teacher. The note read: "Julia does well in school but she could do much better if the pure joy of living did not impede her progress."

April

Tuesday April 1

> I took a day to search for spring,
> And found it through my open door,
> I felt the touch of April's breath
> Luring me . . . wonders to explore.
>
> As I ventured slowly forth,
> A harbinger of spring I spied . . .
> A robin trilled in the balmy air,
> Merrily bursting with song and pride.
>
> Farther down the garden path
> Flowers peeked through the thawing ground,
> Raising fragile spears around the earth,
> So quietly without a sound.
>
> The magic of new blades of grass,
> The green buds on leafless trees,
> Had me awed in wonderment
> Of springtime miracles such as these.
>
> My search for spring was well fulfilled,
> As I viewed the teeming sod,

Resurging life in the new season,
With the helping hand of God.

Have you ever searched for springtime?
If you have not, you cannot know,
The thrill of fresh new buds that bloom,
The caressing winds that blow.

Ann Schneider

Wednesday April 2

My friend Mavis wrote to me from Winnipeg this week. Her letter was interesting as she explained a problem that she had been having with her medication. You see, in the winter Mavis drinks a glass of grapefruit juice every day, hoping that the boost of vitamin C will ward off colds or flu. She didn't realize that the grapefruit juice could cause a problem with the pills she was taking.

As she explained in her letter, grapefruit juice destroys a particular enzyme in the small intestines that is needed to break down a whole host of medications. This can result in the medicine failing to work or, in some cases, working too well, increasing the risk of overdose. As well, several other very common food and drinks and some vitamins and mineral supplements—very healthy when taken on their own—may interact with some blood pressure medications, pain-killers or other remedies.

Fortunately, Mavis called her doctor, and he explained why the grapefruit juice was a problem. He also had some good advice for all of us who take medications regularly. He suggested that you should discuss your diet with your doctor whenever medication is prescribed. As well, your pharmacist can give you detailed information about foods that could interact with your prescription.

As always, if you sense a problem contact your own family physician.

Thursday April 3

One proverb goes something like this: "Fear less, hope more; eat less, chew more; whine less, breathe more; talk less, say more; hate less, love more; and all good things will be yours."

Wise words.

PEONY
Paeonia

Friday April 4

Emily Kimbrough expressed my feelings so well when she said, " 'You haven't changed a bit' is an observation I do not take to kindly. It is a form of greeting prevalent at school reunions, and I have seen its recipients simper with pleasure in a fashion that astonishes me. I have travelled, worked, borne children, lived in various communities and made many more friends than comprised the group that surrounded me in pigtail days, and I hope my looks show something of these experiences. To be told that nothing of this increase in richness and enjoyment of living shows makes me indignant."

Saturday April 5

My grandson Marshall remarked recently, "Nothing is as frustrating as arguing with someone who knows what he's talking about."

Sunday April 6

We beseech thee, Almighty God, mercifully to look upon thy people; that by thy great goodness they may be governed and preserved evermore, both in body and soul; through Jesus Christ, our Lord. Amen

Collect for Passion Sunday
Book of Common Prayer

Monday April 7

My daughter Julia often rents video movies on the weekend. When she recently returned a video, the store manager asked her how she had enjoyed it. She told him that it was good, but not nearly as good as the book. He was somewhat disdainful as he remarked, "Oh . . . you're a reader!"

Tuesday April 8

Kids don't stay with you if you do it right. It's one job where the better you are, the more surely you won't be needed in the long run.

Barbara Kingsolver

My friend Mary McConnell sighed this morning because her son was moving home again, temporarily. He is out of work, and his parents are helping him get on his feet and back into the work force.

"I can't wait until our revolving door at home becomes a one way out, Edna."

With ten children, that might be a while.

Wednesday April 9

Most of us are familiar with the Golden Rule of the Christian faith: do unto others as you would have them do unto you. Many religions have their own versions of this rule, and I present just a few of them to you today.

Hurt not others in ways that you yourself would find hurtful.

Buddhism

This is the sum of all duty: do naught unto others which would cause you pain if done to you.

Islam

In happiness and suffering, in joy and grief, regard all creatures as you would regard you own self.

Jainism

Respect for all life is the foundation.

Native American

That nature alone is good which refrains from doing unto another whatsoever is not good for itself.

Zoroastrianism

What is hateful to you, do not to your fellow man. That is the entire Law; all the rest is commentary.

Judaism

Thursday April 10

My great–grandson Michael is playing hockey this year and is very keen on the game. Happily, he has a coach who is wonderfully enthusiastic and who is working very hard to teach the youngsters basic hockey skills. I think that the coach's attitude is best shown by Michael's response to tonight's question: "How did your game go?"

His answer: "Really great, Grammie! If we had gotten four more goals, we would have beaten them by one goal."

Friday April 11

Millions long for immortality who don't know what to do with themselves on a rainy afternoon.

Susan Ertz

Saturday April 12

Always behave like a duck: keep calm and unruffled on the surface, but paddle like the dickens underneath.

Sunday April 13

Palm Sunday

Ride on! ride on in majesty.
Hark! all the tribes hosanna cry;
O Saviour meek, pursue thy road
With palms and scattered garments strowed.

Ride on! ride on in majesty!
In lovely pomp ride on to die;

Bow thy meek head to mortal pain;
Then take, O God, thy power, and reign.

Dean H. H. Milman

Monday April 14

The deeper man goes into life, the deeper is his conviction that this life is not all; it is an "unfinished symphony." A day may round out an insect's life, and a bird or a beast needs no tomorrow. Not so with him who knows that he is related to God and has felt power of an endless life.

Henry Ward Beecher

Tuesday April 15

A man who wants to do something will find a way; a man who doesn't will find an excuse.

Stephen Dolly Jr.

Wednesday April 16

A gush of bird-song, a patter of dew,
A cloud, and a rainbow's warning,
Suddenly sunshine, and perfect blue . . .
An April day in the morning.

H. P. Sofford

How I love these warmer days of spring! Marg and I went for a walk in the neighbourhood and were delighted to see some crocuses and tulips beginning to bloom. The nicest thing about Easter being in mid- to-late April is that we are able to use flowers from our own garden to decorate our home and the church. This Sunday morning the chancel guild will have many beautiful flowers to remind us of this glorious time of resurrection and renewal.

Thursday April 17

When He came—there was no light; when He left—there was no darkness.

Friday April 18

Good Friday

Then said Jesus, Father, forgive them; for they know not what they do.

Luke 23:34

Saturday April 19

Marg has spent today organizing our Easter dinner. With many of the family joining us tomorrow, she hopes to have most of the work done ahead of time. Peach-glazed ham with fruit compote makes a delicious—and easy—holiday dinner. Serving it with scalloped potatoes and spring green salad prepared earlier will allow Marg to visit with the family instead of spending her time in the kitchen!

Peach-Glazed Ham with Fruit Compote

(may be made several days ahead)

1/2 lb. rhubarb cut in slices (about 2 cups)

4 green onions chopped, white and green parts divided.

1/4 cup sugar

1 tbsp. cider vinegar

1 small can (8 oz.) pineapple, drained and cut into 1/2" pieces

1/2 tsp. ground cinnamon

1/8 tsp. salt

1/2 tsp. pepper

1/4 cup fresh mint

Ham

6–7 lb. shank portion of smoked ham

1/2 cup peach preserves

1/4 cup balsamic vinegar

1/2 tsp. crushed red pepper flakes

Compote

Coat a skillet with cooking spray. Over medium high heat add rhubarb and white part of the onions. Cook, stirring until onion starts to brown (about 2 minutes). Stir in sugar and cook, stirring until rhubarb is tender (about 3–4 minutes). Add next five ingredients. Cook until vinegar evaporates. Remove from heat; cool. Stir in onion greens and mint.

Ham

Preheat oven to 325° F. Place ham on rack in a roasting pan. With a knife, score the fat in a criss-cross pattern about 1/4" deep. Bake 1 hour 15 minutes.

To prepare glaze, bring the preserves, vinegar and pepper flakes to a boil over medium high heat. Reduce heat to medium low; simmer until thickened and reduced to 1/2 cup (about 5 minutes). Brush ham with glaze. Continue baking until meat thermometer, in the thickest portion, registers 140° F. (about 30 minutes). Let ham sit 10 minutes before slicing. Serve with fruit compote.

Serves 12.

Sunday April 20

Easter

He is risen, he is risen,
Tell it with a joyful voice,
He has burst his three days' prison,
Let the whole wide earth rejoice;
Death is conquered, man is free,
Christ has won the victory.

Cecil Frances Alexander

Monday April 21

My grandson Marshall, who is a lawyer, made me laugh today as he told me this story.

SPRING SHOWERS

St. Peter was at the Pearly Gates to welcome two distinguished newcomers. The famous lawyer was shown to a sumptuous suite, beautifully furnished, with a library of fine books and valuable paintings. Then the Pope was shown to his quarters, a sparse room, chilly and bare.

"Hey," said the Pope, "Why is the lawyer's place so much nicer than mine?"

"Well, it's like this," said St. Peter, "We already have more than 100 Popes, and he's our very first lawyer."

Tuesday April 22

Our Lord has written the promise of the Resurrection, not in books alone, but in every leaf in springtime.

Martin Luther

Wednesday April 23

If the day and the night are such that you greet them with joy, and life emits a fragrance like flowers and sweet-scented herbs, is more elastic, more starry, more immortal—that is your success.

Henry David Thoreau

Thursday April 24

So often the young people of today are lumped under the headings of "selfish" or "thoughtless." My great-grandchildren Justin and Jenny, and their high school graduating class, could change many minds with their caring, generous class gift.

With money donated by class members and help from a local nursery, a beautiful garden and seating area is being set up at our local nursing home. The nursery owner will make planting suggestions and supervise as the students lay the patio stones, plant the shrubs and flowers and set up the chairs, benches and umbrella tables that they were able to purchase with the donations.

Jenny explained, "You know, Gram, when we were in middle school, our class used to come and visit for Christmas, Easter and lots of other special occasions. Many of the people living in the home became our friends. Now that we are going off to college or university, we hope that these friends will remember us. We won't be able to visit as often as we used to, but we hope that the garden and visiting area will help them to think of us and the happy times we shared together."

I'm sure that this thoughtful gesture will be greatly appreciated by the residents and staff alike.

Friday April 25

What is it to stay young? It is the ability to hold fast to old friends and to make new ones, to keep forever our beloved in dear remembrance, and to open our hearts quickly to a light knock on the door.

Cornelia Rogers

Saturday April 26
Be glad when spring goes by. . . .
Seek not to stay
Her little laughing feet
Along the way.

Unclasp her April hand
and set her free,
Nor watch her out of sight
Too wistfully.

Be wise and do not hold
Bright Spring too near,
Or you will hunger for
Her touch all year.

Author unknown

Sunday April 27
The mountains shall depart, and the hills be removed; but my kindness shall not depart from thee.

Isaiah 54:10

Monday April 28

Music is the art of the prophets, the only art that can calm the agitations of the soul; it is one of the most magnificent and delightful presents God has given us.

Martin Luther

I was reminded of these words as I watched a special concert by the Boston Symphony Orchestra on television this evening. Hearing the melodic strains of Gershwin's "Rhapsody in Blue" transported me back to a marvelous evening many years ago, when George and I were newlyweds and barely scraping by on his salary as a minister. One of our parishioners gave us tickets to attend a symphony concert in Montreal. We could never have afforded the tickets, so it was an especially wonderful gift. We heard "Rhapsody in Blue" that night and it was a completely magical evening. We could never hear that music again without saying, "Do you remember that concert in Montreal?" It is one of my most beautiful memories.

Tuesday April 29

Nature is the living, visible garment of God.

Goethe

Wednesday April 30

Remember, right is right, even if everyone is against it, and wrong is wrong, even if everyone is for it.

May

Marg and I sat in the sunroom this morning enjoying our tea and looking out at the gardens that are now showing some early growth. I was reminded of these lines from Edna Jacques.

My Grandma's Garden

The flowers of my grandma's day
Were just as fragrant, just as gay;
The bleeding hearts, the larkspur blue,
Did something to the heart of you,
And printed deep in memory's page
The blueprint of your heritage.

A climbing rose that used to peep
Into her room and watch her sleep,
Hollyhocks yellow in the sun
That grew beside the chicken run,
Snapdragons on a steady stem,
And candytuft nod to them.

A snowball tree by the front door
Sprinkled its petals on the floor,
While ragged robins used to vie
With phlox to charm the passerby,

And once a bush of juniper
Broke into lovely bloom for her.

But sweeter than a Sultan's crown
Was grandma in her lilac gown,
Walking among the flowers, knowing
That lavender and rue were growing.
And somehow her old kindly face
Was part and parcel of the place,
Giving it dignity and pride
As if a light were on inside.

Friday May 2

At the park near their home, my friends Will and Muriel were sitting on a bench beside the playground. A gentleman was also on the bench, watching his young son who was on the swing.

"He's a fine-looking boy," Will remarked to the father.

"Thank you," the man replied, and then looking at his watch, he said, "What do you say we go, Mikey?"

Mikey pleaded, "Just five more minutes, please, Daddy?"

The father agreed, and Mikey continued to swing back and forth with obvious delight.

Time passed and Mikey's father called again, "Time to go, son."

"Oh, please, Daddy, just five more minutes?"

The father acquiesced, and the son raced up and down the slide.

The father called a third time, "Ready to go?"

"Just five more minutes, Daddy, ok?" and the father again agreed.

Will remarked to the father, "You're a very patient man."

The man smiled and then explained. "About a year ago our older son, Jeff, was killed by a drunk driver as he rode his bike near here. I didn't spend much time with Jeff, and I would have given anything to have five more minutes with him. I will never make that mistake with Mikey."

Saturday May 3

Who shall explain the extraordinary instinct that tells us, perhaps after a single meeting, that this or that particular person, in some mysterious way, matters to us.

Arthur C. Benson

Sunday May 4

He that dwelleth in the secret place of the most High shall abide under the shadow of the Almighty. I will say of the Lord, He is my refuge and my fortress: my God; in him will I trust.

Psalm 91:1–2

Monday May 5

One of the things we need to do as parents is to let our children handle their failures—be there to support them, but let them handle the disappointing moments. That's how they build their ability to go out on their own and face obstacles. This may not always be the easiest course of action, but it is certainly the best one over the long run.

Tuesday May 6

As I grow older, I have come to realize that almost nothing in this life is more important than our attitude. Our attitude can determine whether we will be a success or a failure; it can be more important than the abilities we have been given because our attitude usually decides how we use our gifts. I remember my dear friend Betty, who was bedridden for many years. She could have become bitter or angry but that was not her choice. She was a wonderful listener and a confidante of many, both young and old. She lived every day with joy and contentment. Her attitude was inspirational.

I offer to you today some other positive ideas on life.

Winning isn't everything, but wanting to win is.
Vince Lombardi

Life is a big canvas, and you should throw all the paint on it you can.

Danny Kaye

It is better to be a lion for a day than to be a sheep all your life.

Sister Kenny

What would life be if we had no courage to attempt anything?

Vincent Van Gogh

Wednesday May 7

My good friend Jake came over for dinner this evening. I enjoy Jake's company very much; we have so many interests in common and his sense of humour always appeals to me.

Jake remarked to me this evening that he has made a list of things he would like to do before he dies. I imagined such things as taking a safari to Africa or climbing the Eiffel Tower.

I laughed out loud when I read his list.

—I'm going to remove the tag on my mattress that says "do not remove under penalty."

—I plan to stroll across the lawn to read the sign that says "do not walk on the grass."

—I'm going to wash my shirt that says "dry clean only."

—I might even undo my seatbelt before the plane comes to a complete stop.

"We old folks can live dangerously, Edna."

Thursday May 8

When things are bad, we take comfort in the thought that they could always be worse. And when they are, we find hope in the thought that things are so bad they have to get better.

Malcom S. Forbes

Friday May 9

My coat and I live comfortably together. It has assumed all my wrinkles, does not hurt me anywhere, has molded itself on my deformities, is complacent to all my movements, and I only feel its presence because it keeps me warm. Old coats and friends are the same thing.

Victor Hugo

Saturday May 10

My son-in-law John is often asked to speak at various functions. Most often his time is graciously donated, but on other occasions he is paid an honorarium. He often likes to begin his talks with this story of the late Isaac Asimov, noted American author and speaker.

Mr. Asimov was about to begin his speech

when the gentleman who was introducing him asked if he could read correspondence that had been exchanged about the terms under which Asimov would speak. Mr. Asimov, not remembering the details, agreed. As it turned out, the committee had offered an amount that was about half of the minimum that Asimov would normally receive. His letter of reply (now read by the chairman) said: "Since I am at least twice as good as the average speaker you will get, I want twice the fee you offer. You will see that I'm worth the extra money when I talk to your group." He then sat down and left Asimov to face an audience that now knew that they had paid twice their regular fee to hear him.

Sunday May 11

Mother's Day

I thank the unknown author for these lines for today.

I gave you life
    but I cannot live it for you.
I can teach you things
    but I cannot make you learn.
I can give you direction
    but I cannot always be there to lead you.
I can allow you freedom
    but I cannot account for it.

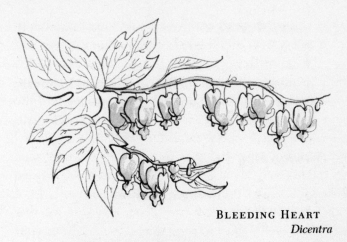

BLEEDING HEART
Dicentra

I can take you to church
  but I cannot make you believe.
I can teach you right from wrong
  but I cannot always decide for you.
I can buy you beautiful clothes
  but I cannot make you lovely inside.
I can offer you my advice
  but I cannot accept it for you.
I can give you my love
  but I cannot force it upon you.
I can teach you kindness
  but I cannot force you to be gracious.
I can warn you about sins
  but I cannot make your morals.
I can love you as a child
  but I cannot place you in God's family.
I can pray for you
  but I cannot make you walk with God.

Monday May 12

Life is made up, not of great sacrifices or duties, but of little things. Smiles and kindnesses and small obligations given habitually preserve the heart and secure comfort.

Sir H. Davy

Tuesday May 13

Enduring Things

And what, then
  is the all important goal
To which we drive ourselves
  and have no time
To listen to the singing of the soul,
  Or rise on spirit wings to thoughts sublime?
One day the world will grind
  much as before
Without our grim direction,
  and the wheels
Will somehow turn
  when we have passed the door
That leads beyond four walls
  and three square meals.
And what then will we have to take along
Where there are neither pockets,
vaults nor shelves,
When all that we can hold
  will be our song

And what we worked to build
  into ourselves?
Oh, listen to the universe that sings
Through hearts attuned to Life's enduring
  things.

Mary E. Linton

Wednesday May 14

If you don't think every day is a good day, try
missing one.

Cavett Robert

Thursday May 15

For many years my husband George sub-
scribed to the *Saturday Evening Post* magazine. The *Post* was interesting and informative,
but more often than not, George most enjoyed
the Norman Rockwell cover illustrations.

Norman Rockwell was born in February 1894.
He left high school to study at the Art Students'
League with George Bridgeman and Thomas
Fogarty.

Rockwell specialized in depictions of small
town life and its ordinary people. One of the
most noticeable characteristics of his work was a
meticulous detailing of clothing and accessories.

People loved his work because his love for the
people he painted was so obvious. In a 1923
issue of *International Studio*, he said, "People

somehow get out of your work just what you put into it, and if you're interested in the characters you draw, and understand and love them, why, the person who sees your picture will feel the same way." George and I enjoyed all of Rockwell's work, but a particular favourite was *Grace*, an image depicting a young boy and his mother giving thanks for their meal in a truck stop diner. Rockwell's work is sure to be enjoyed for generations to come.

Friday May 16

After all the great religions have been preached and expounded, or have been revealed in brilliant scholars, or have been written in fine books and embellished in fine language with finer covers, man—all man—is still confronted with The Great Mystery.

Chief Luther Standing Bear
Oglala Sioux

Saturday May 17

Well, today is "D" day (as in diet start day) at our house. Dieting has become a yearly ritual as my son-in-law Bruce realizes that his summer wear is uncomfortably tight after a long winter of eating comfort foods.

As of today, my daughter Marg and I expect to hear many moans and sighs as Bruce complains of missing his "real" food, but to give him credit, once he has decided to lose weight, he has great willpower and will stick to a regimen until he reaches his goal.

As Bruce pointed out, "Dieting is that time when you can eat as much as you like, but only of the foods you don't like."

Sunday May 18

Every good gift and every perfect gift is from above, and cometh down from the Father of lights, with whom is no variableness, neither shadow of turning.

James 1:17

Monday May 19

Marg, Bruce and I have enjoyed a beautiful weekend—the traditional cottage opening—here in Muskoka at my dear friend Eleanor's summer home.

Many years ago, after Eleanor's husband passed away, she was overwhelmed at the thought of opening the cottage on her own. Bruce immediately offered to take on the more difficult physical chores . . . turning on the water, checking the pipes, putting the boat in the lake, taking down the shutters. Marg, Eleanor and I dust, vacuum, put on fresh bedding and mop the floors. Between the four of us we are able to ready the cottage for the summer in just a few days.

We all love the Muskoka area so much that it scarcely seems like work. Whenever we need a break, we take our tea on the porch and breath in the clear air of this magnificent place.

At the turn of the century, Algernon Black-wood, the British writer, wrote of his visit here: "The Muskoka interlude remained for me a sparkling, radiant memory, alight with the sunshine of unclouded skies, with the gleam of stars in a blue-black heaven."

Tonight we'll see those self-same stars and be dazzled by their beauty and by the "blue-black heaven."

Tuesday May 20

Resiliency is an important factor in living. The winds of life may bend us, but if we have resilience of spirit, they cannot break us. To courageously straighten again after our heads have been bowed by defeat, disappointment and suffering is the supreme test of character.

Wednesday May 21

On this day back in 1927, a young American climbed into a small aircraft and made a journey that would put him into the annals of aviation history.

Charles Augustus Lindberg was 25 years old when he boarded his small monoplane, *The Spirit of St. Louis*, and took off from Roosevelt

Field in New York. Thirty-three and one-half hours later, he landed at Le Bourget airport in Paris, the first person to successfully cross the Atlantic. The $25,000 prize offered for the first transatlantic crossing was his.

His exploit caused a world-wide sensation, and "Lindy" became a national hero. It seems hard to imagine that 76 years have passed since that amazing day.

Thursday May 22

What do we live for, if it is not to make life less difficult for others?

George Eliot

Friday May 23

A conscience, like a buzzing bee, can make a fellow feel uneasy without ever stinging him.

Saturday May 24

This is a delightful time of year to visit the orchards of the Niagara region. Marg and Bruce took me and my dear friend Lila on just such a visit today.

Instead of taking the main highway, Bruce chose to use the back roads, giving us a much closer look at many of the fruit farms and vineyards in this area. The beauty of the blossoms was breathtaking.

The pink and white blossom-covered branches,

as well as the mauve and red variety, foretell an abundant harvest to come.

We enjoyed lunch at a small restaurant in Niagara-on-the-Lake and then a restful back-roads drive home.

It was a particularly nice outing for Lila, because she now resides in a nursing home and, without close family living nearby, her sorties are infrequent. We were both very grateful to Marg and Bruce for a lovely day.

Many blessings do the advancing years bring with them.

Horace

For Lila and me, the love of Marg and Bruce is one of our blessings.

Sunday May 25

Then God said, Let the earth put forth vegetation, plants yielding seed, and fruit trees of every kind on earth that bear fruit with the seed in it. And it was so. The earth brought forth vegetation: plants yielding seed of every kind, and trees of every kind bearing fruit with the seed in it. And God saw that it was good.

Genesis 1:11–12

Monday May 26

This is Memorial Day, celebrated by our neighbours to the south in the United Sates. Originally, it was a day set aside to honour those who died in service to their country. Now it has evolved into a day to honour all those friends and relatives who have passed from this life.

I believe that when the soul disappears from the world, it disappears only to become manifest upon another scene in the wondrous drama of eternity.

Edwin Markham

Tuesday May 27

Evan Esar, an American humourist, once remarked, "The advantage of living on a farm is that cows and chickens don't come in and urge you to play bridge when you'd rather read."

Wednesday May 28

On this date in 1914, one of Canada's greatest marine disasters occurred in the St. Lawrence River.

On a mild afternoon, the *Empress of Ireland*, queen of the Canadian Pacific Line, set off from the pier below Quebec's Chateau Frontenac hotel. On board the liner were 1,479 passengers, many of whom were members of the Salvation

MAY FLOWERS

Army en route to the international congress in London.

The ship sailed down river toward the Atlantic Ocean. Sharing the foggy night and the river with the *Empress* was the Norwegian coaler *Storstadt*, carrying 10,000 tons of coal. The chief officer saw the lights but calculated that he would pass port to port. In fact he was aimed right at the *Empress*, and he slammed into her amidships, all but cutting her in two.

It was immediately apparent to the *Empress*' captain, George Kendall, that his ship was sinking. The order was given to abandon ship, but it took only 14 minutes for this great liner to sink, leaving the passengers and crew struggling in the freezing water.

Despite the fact that the *Empress* was in sight of shore and safety when the collision occurred, few survived, and 1,012 of the passengers were listed as dead or missing. This disaster of unprecedented proportions in Canada's history is a story not yet well known or often told.

Thursday May 29

Some men have their first dollar. The man who is really rich is one who still has his first friend.

Friday May 30

Kind hearts are the garden—
Kind thoughts are the roots—

Kind words are the flowers—
Kind deeds are the fruit.

Saturday May 31
To analyse the charm of flowers is like dissecting music; it is one of those things which it is far better to enjoy than to attempt fully to understand.

Henry T. Tuckerman

June

Sunday June 1

O heavenly father, in whom we live and move and have our being: We humbly pray thee so to guide and govern us by thy Holy Spirit, that in all the cares and occupations of our life we may not forget thee, but may remember that we are ever walking in thy sight; through Jesus Christ our Lord. Amen.

A Collect for Guidance
Book of Common Prayer

Monday June 2

My husband, George, and I shared a wonderful and happy marriage. Although we were very young when we married, and George's salary was meager, we seemed to be rich in so many other ways.

Yesterday was the anniversary of our marriage, and I thank the unkown author for these lines which have so much meaning for me.

Time cannot steal the treasure
That we carry in our hearts,
Nor dim the shining thoughts
Our cherished past imparts.

And memories of the ones we've loved
Still cast their gentle glow,
To grace our days and light our paths
Wherever we may go.

Tuesday June 3

Few people in this world work harder than the farmer. Their hours are exceptionally long, and much of the success of the crop depends on the weather. My sister, Sarah, lives in a farming community on Canada's east coast. I laughed as I remembered this story from some years ago.

A young doctor opened his practice in a rural area of New Brunswick. He was awakened on his second morning by the ringing of his doorbell at 4:30 a.m. As he stumbled in the dark toward the door, he was scrambling to clear his mind for what he assumed must be a terrible emergency. When he opened the door, he was surprised to see a farmer, looking quite fit.

"Good heavens man, what is it?" the doctor asked urgently.

"Why nothing much, doctor," replied the farmer. "You asked me to drop by for my blood test before breakfast, and here I am."

Wednesday June 4

One of the annoying things about weather forecasts is that they are not wrong all the time, either.

Thursday June 5

> And what is so rare as a day in June?
> Then, if ever, come perfect days;
> Then Heaven tries the earth if it be in tune
> And over it softly her warm ear lays.
>
> *James Russell Lowell*

In our area, June really does seem to have more perfect days than the other months. Warmer days and nights than April or May, but not the steamy or uncomfortable times of July and August, make the 30 days of June some of the most enjoyable of the year.

My friend Lila and I enjoyed tea on the terrace today and talked of other lovely days in Junes past. It truly is a magical time of the year!

Friday June 6

A professor at Oxford University offered this sage advice:

"Nothing you learn here at Oxford will be of the slightest possible use to you later, save only this: that if you work hard and intelligently, you should be able to detect when a man is talking rot. And that, in my view, is the main, if not the sole, purpose of education."

Saturday June 7

The measure of a man's life is the well spending of it, and not the length.

Plutarch

Sunday June 8

Faith of our fathers! living still
In spite of dungeons, fire and sword;
O how our hearts beat high with joy
When e'er we hear that glorious word!
Faith of our fathers! Holy faith!
We will be true to thee till death!

Rev. F. W. Faber

Monday June 9

On this, my birthday, I am reminded of the lines, "For all within is young, and glowing, in spite of old age's outward showing."

Tuesday June 10

At this time of year, one of my favourite fruits is ready to be picked. Is there anything that can beat the taste of a ripe red strawberry picked and eaten right there in the field?

Many farms in our area feature "pick your own" berries, where visitors take their baskets into the field and select the choicest of the fruits to take home.

Our family has what seems to be an endless

supply of strawberry recipes, so as well as a wonderful afternoon picking berries together, we are able to spend time sharing our cooking "secrets." I heartily recommend this enjoyable pastime.

Wednesday June 11

I thank my friend Marcia for sending me these lines for today.

If you have learned to walk
A little more sure-footed than I,
Be patient with my stumbling then
And know that only as I do my best and try
May I attain my goal
For which we are both striving.

If through experience your soul
Has gained heights which I
As yet in dim-lit vision see,
Hold out you hand and point the way
Lest from its straightness I should stray
And walk a mile with me.

Author unknown

Thursday June 12

My brother Ben is a gardener and he looks forward each spring to those hours spent nurturing the plants and flowers that grow in such abundance under his green thumb.

Ben has several friends who also enjoy gardening but have found that the limitations of their advancing age and decreased strength have made their cherished task of gardening very difficult.

Fortunately for them, Ben, who spends most winter evenings reading gardening journals, has been able to help them switch their gardens to the low maintenance variety using ground covers and perennials. Once again they will enjoy that calmness of spirit that seems to be a part of all those who work in gardens.

Friday June 13

A little nonsense now and then
Is relished by the wisest men.

Old Proverb

Saturday June 14

The soon-to-arrive summer is even more apparent as the early fruits and vegetables make their way to the outdoor farmers' markets. In our area, the farmers' market opens on the long weekend in May and remains open each weekend until the end of October. Main Street is blocked off each Saturday morning at 6 a.m., and farmers set up stalls that feature such items as meat, fish, eggs, cheese and a multitude of freshly picked fruits and vegetables. We like to arrive early and enjoy hot apple cider and bacon-on-a-bun for breakfast. Arriving around 7:30 a.m. gives us a chance to meet with friends and neighbours who also enjoy an early start to their Saturday.

Sunday June 15

Father's Day

I think that one of the finest tributes any man can receive is to hear his children say, "He's a wonderful father."

This, from William Hamilton Hayne, says it well:

To My Father

It matters not that Time has shed
His thawless snow upon your head,
For he maintains, with wondrous art,
Perpetual summer in your heart.

Monday June 16

My dear friend Muriel celebrated her birthday this weekend. Muriel is one of those people we would describe as aging gracefully, someone who embraces each day and becomes more lovely with each passing year.

Many people have spoken of growing old, and I offer some of those thoughts today.

Beautiful young people are accidents of nature.
But beautiful old people are works of art.

M. B. Greenbie

Don't be ashamed of your gray hair! Wear it
proudly like a flag ... Grow old eagerly, triumphantly!

It is magnificent to grow old, if one keeps young.

Henry Emerson Fosdick

Some lives, like evening primroses, blossom
most beautifully in the evening of life.

C. E. Corman

Tuesday June 17

Our family is very excited as we celebrate my
great-grandchildren's happy news of today.
Justin and Jenny received letters of acceptance
from university and are thrilled to have been
accepted at their first choices.

Over the years, Justin and Jenny have been so
fortunate to have had excellent teachers—indi-
viduals who have given unsparingly of their time,
been understanding of the needs of all students,
and have demanded only the best from each.

I offer this poem, "Our Teacher ... Our
Friend," to all those teachers who have enriched
the lives of my great-grandchildren.

God gave to you that rarest gift,
An understanding heart
A gentle, kindly manner
Your wisdom to impart.

O some men build with steel and iron,
To pave their way to fame,
But you are building character
A lasting tribute to your name.

The lives you touch, the good you do
Shall never know an end,
And we are proud to call you . . .
Our teacher and our friend.

Wednesday June 18

I laughed at John's story today. Young Bobby, scolded for being naughty, was asked by his mother, "How do you expect to get into heaven?"

He thought for a moment, then replied, "Well, I'll just run in and out and keep slamming the door until they say, 'For goodness sake, come in or stay out!' Then I'll go in."

Thursday June 19

If you would have your son be something in this world, teach him to depend on himself. Let him learn that it is by close and strenuous personal application he must rise—that he must, in short, make himself, and be the architect of his own fortune.

Howard Edwards

Friday June 20

Every man, woman and child on this earth has an overwhelming desire to be loved, to be wanted, to be appreciated. To the extent that we can fulfill this desire will we give happiness and find happiness in ourselves.

Saturday June 21

We welcomed summer's arrival with a bar-beque this evening. Marshall made some wonderful blue-cheese-stuffed burgers with hot sauce. I left the hot sauce to the young folks, but the burgers were delicious!

Hamburgers with Hot Sauce

2 lbs. ground beef
2 drops Tabasco sauce
1/2 tsp. salt
1/4 tsp. cayenne
1/4 tsp. pepper
6 tbsp. blue cheese, divided

In a bowl mix beef, Tabasco, salt, cayenne and pepper. Divide the mixture into 12 portions; flatten into 4" patties. Make a well in the centre of 6 patties and place 1 tbsp. of blue cheese in the centre of each indentation. Top with remaining six patties and pinch the edges to seal. Grill the burgers, turning once, 5–6 minutes per side for medium. Serve on buns with hot sauce (if desired), lettuce, onion slices, pickles and tomato.

Hot Sauce

3 tbsp. butter or margarine
2 cloves garlic, minced
1 tbsp. + 1 tsp. vinegar
1 tbsp. Worcestershire sauce
1 tsp. Tabasco sauce
1/2 tsp. salt
1/2 tsp. cayenne
1/4 tsp. pepper
1/2 cup ketchup

Melt the butter in a small pot over medium-high heat. Add garlic, vinegar, Worcestershire sauce, Tabasco, salt, cayenne and pepper. Cook until garlic softens (about 1 minute). Stir in ketchup, and bring to a boil. Reduce heat to medium. Simmer for 6 – 8 minutes until slightly thickened, stirring occasionally.

Serve with burgers.

Sunday June 22

I love the Lord, because He hath heard my voice and my supplications. Because he hath inclined his ear unto me, therefore will I call upon him as long as I live.

Psalm 116:1–2

Monday June 23

Bruce came home this evening in rather bad humour. He and several friends had played golf after work today, and he had not played at all well.

He gave us a blow-by-blow account of each shot, sighing deeply all the while.

"Well dear, perhaps you should give up playing golf if it upsets you so," Marg suggested.

Bruce's reaction was predictable. "Give it up? Good heavens, Marg, I love golfing! Why would I give it up?"

Over dinner, Bruce told us of a game once played by Mark Twain with Woodrow Wilson, future president on the United States.

Mr. Wilson caught the turf under one of his drives, sending grass and dirt in all directions.

To hide his embarrassment, he remarked heartily, "I hope you're enjoying our links here, Mark."

Twain spit out the dirt that had hit him in the face and answered with his usual flair, "I'll say this for them, Woodrow, they're the best I have ever tasted."

Tuesday June 24

Many Canadians know that today is St. Jean Baptiste Day, celebrated in Quebec and in French-speaking communities from coast to coast. Fewer people probably know that on this day in 1497 the explorer John Cabot landed on the coast of Newfoundland.

I'm sure that our friends in both provinces will be celebrating today. A happy day to all!

Wednesday June 25

The month of June was usually the busiest one in the life of a minister and his family. Along with the many weddings that were a tradition in June, two other important social events took place. One was the church picnic and the other was the strawberry social. In most small parishes, the strawberry social was (and still is) a marvelous fundraiser. The ladies of the church set up long tables and covered them with sparkling white sheets (which they called tablecloths) and set about serving the best strawberry shortcake ever made.

Many rural churches still hold the strawberry social, and if you enjoy these wonderful berries you need not look too far to find a spot to enjoy a delicious shortcake and perhaps meet new friends.

Thursday June 26

It seems to me we can never give up longing and wishing while we are thoroughly alive. There are certain things we feel to be beautiful and good, and we must hunger after them.

George Eliot

Friday June 27

Edith Wharton, author of such great books as *Ethan Frome* and *The Age of Innocence*, was never given much encouragement by her relatives. In fact they considered writing books no fit occupation for a lady of quality.

An uncle of hers once remarked that he considered Miss Wharton to be slightly more erratic than another unfortunate relative who "spent his last years sitting on a marble shelf in the happy illusion that he was a bust of Napoleon."

Thankfully, Miss Wharton took no notice of her relations.

Saturday June 28

Come walk with me along this willowed lane,
Where, like lost coinage from some miser's store
The golden dandelions more and more
Glow as the warm sun kisses them again.

Henry Sylvester Cornwell

Sunday June 29

Now learn a parable of the fig tree; When his branch is yet tender, and putteth forth leaves, ye know that summer is nigh.

Mathew 24:32

Monday June 30

Faced with a difficult problem, many of us may feel overwhelmed. Ruth Stafford Peale (wife of Norman Vincent Peale, minister and author) offered this story that has helped her see difficult situations more clearly.

"Some years ago, the lovely old maple tree in our yard had died. Norman and I were both crestfallen as we surveyed it one Saturday morning. 'I guess we'd better call the man,' Norman said. 'It's too close to the house for comfort!'

"The tree surgeon came that afternoon but instead of sawing through the trunk immediately, as we expected, he began by trimming away small upper branches. Then he sawed off the larger limbs until just the lower trunk was left. Then he sectioned this too, until his final cut, when the tree base toppled harmlessly to the ground. 'On difficult jobs like these,' he explained, 'we always tackle the easy part first. That way the rest of the problem gets simpler and simpler as we go along.'

"Now, whenever I am stymied by a sticky problem, I think back to that Saturday. Instead of trying to cope with the whole dilemma at once, I have learned to sort it into little pieces that aren't so hard to tackle after all."

What wise advice.

July

Tuesday July 1
"Oh Canada, our home and native land."

Today we celebrate the birth of our nation back in 1867. With the signing of the Articles of Confederation, this magnificent country called Canada came into being.

When the Fathers of Confederation were preparing the foundations for our country, one of the problems they faced was deciding on the name. Some of the suggestions were Laurentia, Ursalia, Mesopelagia, Albionora, Borealia, Colonia, Hochelaga, Efisga, Tuponia and Canada.

When the explorer Jacques Cartier asked the Iroquois the name of their land, the answer given was "Canada." Historians now believe that this word meant "a collection of huts" and that the aboriginals thought Cartier was asking about their nearby village.

Today we celebrate the 136th birthday with immense pride.

Wednesday July 2
Knowledge is a comfortable and necessary retreat and shelter for us in an advanced

age; and if we do not plant it while young, it will give us no shade when we grow old.

Lord Chesterfield

Thursday July 3

I find summer days to be so relaxing. The hazy warmth just makes me feel like sitting in the shade of a tree and reading.

Luckily for me, my friend Lila often has the same inclination, and we two head to the beautiful patio area of the nursing home where she lives.

Marg often drops me off just after lunch, and Lila and I sit in the shade of the large maple tree. The comfortable chairs and a large pitcher of icy cold lemonade make just about the perfect place to be on a summer afternoon.

There is something so agreeable about a companionable silence when reading with a friend. We often go for hours without speaking, but on those occasions that we feel like chatting, we have someone with whom we can share our thoughts.

A friend may well be reckoned the masterpiece of nature.

Ralph Waldo Emerson

Friday July 4

Our American friends are celebrating Independence Day. It is, for them, a day of inspiration and renewal—a day to enjoy the "inalienable right to the pursuit of happiness."

Virginia K. Oliver's poem, "The Fourth of July," is a fine tribute for this day.

I love the patriotism
Of the Fourth of July,
All the celebration
And the flags flying high.

I like the independence
And glory of this day,
With the meaning of true freedom
For our U.S.A.

I remember our forefathers . . .
That memory shall not fade
Of their great and gallant courage
Of which history is made.

Then I look into the future
And with such pride do I
Think on the eternal triumph
Of the fourth of July!

Saturday July 5

Life is like an onion; you pull one layer at a time and sometimes you weep.

PETUNIA

Sunday July 6

Thou visitest the earth and waterest it: thou greatly enrichest it.

They drop upon the pastures of the wilderness: and the little hills rejoice on every side.

The pastures are clothed with flocks; the valleys also are covered over with corn; they shout for joy, they also sing.

Psalm 65:9, 12–13

Monday July 7

As we grow older, I think that all of us hope that we grow wiser. A number of my friends and I came up with this list of important things we have learned over these many years. I'm sure that you could come up with many more.

I've learned . . . that you view other people's children in a whole different light when you have some of your own.

I've learned . . . that being kind is much more important than being right.

I've learned . . . no matter their ages or how far away they may be, you never stop wanting to protect your children.

I've learned . . . no matter your age, you can feel like a child of twelve when your mother is talking to you.

I've learned . . . the less time I have, the more I seem to get done.

I've learned . . . if you run through life too fast, you forget not only where you've been, but also where you're going.

Tuesday July 8

Labour to keep alive in your heart that little spark of celestial fire called conscience.

George Washington

Wednesday July 9

What a wonderful celebration we had today. Phyllis and Bill were married twenty years ago on this date, and two years later, their children, Justin and Jenny, were born. It hardly seems possible that these years passed so quickly and that the twins will be off to university in the fall.

Because this was such a significant anniversary, Phyllis and Bill wanted many friends and family members to join them in their celebration. They had a large tent set up in the back yard, and it was decorated with hundreds of tiny white Christmas lights. Flowers from their garden were on each of the tables, and a local caterer provided a delicious meal of summer salads. Justin and Jenny also had a large number of friends attend, and one young man provided music of a delightful variety . . . everything from Frank Sinatra to Elvis Presley, from big-band swing to today's most popular sounds.

Sitting back and watching the generations mingle and enjoy each other's company was such fun.

I couldn't help but think how proud George would have been!

Thursday July 10

I thank the unknown author for these lines today.

Walk a Country Mile

I like to walk a country mile
On a pleasant summer's day,
Enjoying the many sights and sounds
I find along the way.

I hear the song the meadow brook
Sings to me as I pass by,
And watch the birds so wild and free,
Soar swiftly 'neath an azure sky.

I wander up a hillside trail,
And see the fields below arranged
All criss-crossed lying o'er the earth
So like a patchwork counterpane.

I pass a meadow, green and wide,
Where cattle graze in shaded space,
And ducklings in the summer sun,
Pass single file in measured pace.

I like to walk a country mile
And no matter where I roam,
My heart is filled with gladness,
For the country is my home.

Friday July 11

Some people see more in a walk around the block than others see in a trip around the world.

Saturday July 12

One of my favorite treats on a warm summer evening is an ice-cream cone. We have a wonderful ice-cream parlour within walking distance, and Marg, Bruce and I will often stroll down to the mill pond and then make our way back to the parlour to enjoy a delicious cool treat.

You might be interested to know that, according to one authority, the first ice-cream was made thousands of years ago when someone inadvertently left a bowl of milk outside on a cold night. More than 3000 years ago, the Chinese mixed snow and fruit juices to make desserts. In the fourth century, Alexander the Great enjoyed ice-cream made from honey, fruit juices and milk, which was frozen with snow and carried down from the mountains by relays of slaves.

Ice-cream was popular in Europe in the 1500s and 1600s, and was enjoyed by well-to-do colonists in America. In 1864, an American woman, Nancy Johnson, invented the hand-cranked freezer.

What a delicious progression from that one bowl of frozen milk to the many hundreds of flavours that are offered today all around the world!

Sunday July 13

Train up a child in the way he should go: and when he is old, he will not depart from it.

Proverbs 22:6

Monday July 14

The beauty of the world and the orderly arrangement of everything celestial makes us confess that there is an excellent and eternal nature, which ought to be worshipped and admired by all of mankind.

Cicero

Tuesday July 15

Life is made up of adjustments, both the little ones in everyday living, and the larger ones that come only occasionally. The manner in which we accept these adjustments will determine whether we are happy and serene or discontented.

Wednesday July 16

Happy is the man who can enjoy the small things, the common beauties, the little day-by-day events; sunshine on the fields, birds on the bough, breakfast, dinner, supper, the daily paper on the porch, a friend passing by.

So many people who go afield for enjoyment leave it behind them at home.

David Grayson

Thursday July 17

My friend Jake Frampton is heading to Canada's east coast for a holiday. Jake and his nephew Peter are planning to travel the "lighthouse route" in Nova Scotia, a journey that will take them from Peggy's Cove to Yarmouth. On this route they will pass through a number of weathered fishing villages along a rugged coastline where they will take in the sights, sounds and smells that are the quintessence of Nova Scotia.

Peggy's Cove, about 50 kilometers south of Halifax, is probably best known for its lighthouse, which has been one of the most photographed landmarks in Canada. Peggy's Cove has neat wooden houses and many colourful fishing boats that have drawn artists like magnets.

Lunenburg, Nova Scotia's premier fishing port, is one of the few places on the continent where traditional boat building is still practiced. Lunenburg is also the home of *Bluenose II*, a ship modelled after the fastest fishing schooner ever built. The town has narrow, hilly streets lined with many old homes gaily painted in bright red, white, blue and yellow. It also boasts a number of excellent restaurants and distinctive shops.

Farther west on the route are the towns of Liverpool, Mahone Bay and Shelburne.

At the end of the lighthouse route is Yarmouth, a community featuring many grand mansions built in the nineteenth century by wealthy bankers, lawyers and sea captains.

I'm sure that Jake and Peter will enjoy an unforgettable trip!

Friday July 18

My daughter Mary and her husband, John, stopped on their way home from a party. It was, according to John, an extremely dull affair and he was happy to have left quite early. After listening to John, I was reminded of this amusing story.

Many years ago, Alexander Woollcott and a friend were attending an extremely dull party. After about half an hour they could stand it no longer and made a hasty exit.

"Whew, that was boring!" muttered his friend. Woollcott, in characteristic style, added, "Now that we've left, it must be ghastly!"

Saturday July 19

There are two statements about human beings that are true: that all human beings are alike, and that all human beings are different. On those two facts all human wisdom is founded.

Mark Van Doren

Sunday July 20

For the beauty of the earth,
For the glory of the skies,
For the love which from our birth,

Over and around us lies,
Lord of all to thee we raise,
This our grateful psalm of praise.

F. S. Pierpoint

Monday July 21

When our girls were young, July was the month that George took for his vacation. For many years George would offer to replace other vacationing ministers in various parishes in the country. Our accommodation was supplied, usually a small cottage on the lake, and it meant that the girls, George and I had the chance to relax and spend time with each other. George would preach at the Sunday morning services, but the rest of the time was ours to enjoy.

We were lucky enough to go to the same parish for a number of summers. We made several close friends in the area, and the girls had many other youngsters with whom they could enjoy the simple pleasures of summer at the lake. Some of these cottage friends remain close to this day.

We have many wonderful memories of those cottage days, but the summer that we recollect most clearly was the one where almost anything that could go wrong did.

The cottage where we stayed was on an island, but the boat that was our transportation back and forth to the mainland leaked and the motor

LAZY DAYS
OF SUMMER

would frequently quit—usually while it was raining.

The roof leaked, the mice were so comfortable they almost became pets, the water pump worked only sporadically and it rained more than any other summer that I remember.

We popped popcorn, played cards or monopoly and laughed at every disaster that occurred.

Ah, memories!

Tuesday July 22

Real happiness is more a habit than a goal, more of an attitude than an attainment. It is the companion of cheerfulness, not the creature of circumstances. Happiness is what overtakes us when we forget ourselves, when we learn to open our eyes in optimism and close the door in the face of defeat.

William Arthur Ward

Wednesday July 23

Today is Marg and Bruce's wedding anniversary. I offer for them today this exquisite poem from Elizabeth Barrett Browning.

How Do I Love Thee?

How do I love thee? Let me count the ways.
I love thee to the depth and breadth and
   height
My soul can reach, when feeling out of sight

For the ends of Being and ideal Grace.
I love thee to the level of every day's
Most quiet need, by sun and candle-light.
I love thee freely, as men strive for right;
I love thee purely, as they turn from praise.
I love thee with the passion put to use
In my old griefs, and with my childhood's
  faith.
I love thee with a love I seemed to lose
With my lost saints, I love thee with the
  breath,
Smiles, tears, of all my life!—and, if God
  choose,
I shall but love thee better after death.

Thursday July 24

My grandson Marshall and his family own a sailboat, and most evenings and weekends they can be found out on the waters of Lake Ontario.

The yacht club of which they are members runs a very special program, and both Marshall and his wife Jamie are instructors (on a volunteer basis). Once a week a group of mentally and physically handicapped people boards a sailboat where they receive their first taste of sailing. By the end of just a few weeks, they have learned proper crewing techniques and sailing etiquette, and their level of confidence has grown dramatically.

The yacht club members are justifiably proud of the program.

Happiness adds and multiplies as we divide it with others.

Friday July 25

George Meredith, when speaking of sportsmanship, said, "Always imitate the behaviour of the winners when you lose."

Saturday July 26

So long as enthusiasm lasts, so long is youth still with us.

Sunday July 27

Behold us Lord, a little space
From daily tasks set free,
And met within the holy place
To rest awhile with thee.

Rev. John Ellerton

Monday July 28

An entrepreneur is the kind of person who will work 16 hours a day just to avoid having to work 8 hours for someone else.

Tuesday July 29

Our friends Will and Muriel have a magnificent, lush, green lawn. Will labours tirelessly over it from early spring on, and the result of his tender care is the nicest lawn in the neighbourhood.

Will likes to tell the story of a friend who visited one of the colleges at Oxford University in England.

The visitor commented that he greatly admired the immaculate, lush lawn. He wondered aloud how such perfection had been achieved, and the groundskeeper was summoned to explain to Will's friend how the college had attained such a magnificent growth.

The groundskeeper's reply was typically British.

"Well sir, we mow east and west for two hundred years. Then we mow north and south for two hundred years. Then we change about again."

Wednesday July 30

Some of the youngsters in our neighbourhood have returned from summer camp. One of the young Simpson girls was telling me that, at her camp, they were offered a choice at every meal. The choice: take it or leave it.

Thursday July 31

Money and time are the heaviest burdens of life, and the unhappiest of all mortals are those who have more of either than they know how to use.

August

Friday August 1

I chose these lovely lines from Percy Bysshe Shelley for the rainy first day of August.

The Cloud

I bring fresh showers for the thirsty flowers
From the seas and the streams;
I bear light shade for the leaves when laid
In their noonday dreams.
From my wings are shaken the dews that
    waken
The sweet buds every one,
When rocked to rest on their mother's breast,
As she dances about the sun.
I wield the flail of the lashing hail,
And whiten the green pastures under,
And then again I dissolve it in rain,
And I laugh as I pass in thunder.

Saturday August 2

Maturity is when you realize how much you thought you knew, but didn't.

Sunday August 3

O Father, my hope.
O Son, my refuge.
O Holy Spirit, my protection.
Holy Trinity, glory to Thee.
Compline—St. Joannikios

Eastern Orthodox

Monday August 4

Because advances in health science allow so many of us to live much longer, making every effort to age successfully is important. Many factors are involved in the process, but it seems we must adhere to four basic principles: enjoy a variety of meaningful activities, practice good health habits (exercise and proper nutrition), use sound financial planning and finally, keep an optimistic attitude.

According to experts, the happiest older people are those who have a balance of different kinds of activities—group, solitary, active, passive, indoor, outdoor. Being a part of a group boosts esteem and is a major positive factor in the life of most elderly people. Family is an important group to maintain, but peer group contacts are also crucial as we get older.

Financial planning is essential and also must be started early in life. Professional help may assist in wise choices.

An optimistic outlook can add years to your

SUMMER GARDEN

life. People who adjust to such difficult changes as retirement, health problems, even widowhood, are able to be happy in their later years.

With the proper mental outlook, good health care and intelligent planning, we can look forward to enjoying our "golden years."

Tuesday August 5

Some years ago, former U.S. president Gerald Ford was commencement speaker at his daughter's graduation from high school.

"You might be interested to know that my daughter, Susan, gave me some advice on this speech," the President began. "She asked me not to talk too long, not to tell any jokes, not to talk about her and not to talk about the way things were when I was your age. So, in conclusion . . ."

Wednesday August 6

The reason that many people don't climb the ladder of success is that they're waiting for the elevator.

Thursday August 7

Jake Frampton is enjoying his trip to Nova Scotia very much. He and Peter were in Lunenburg when he wrote, and they were both very intrigued by some of the lore in this historic old village.

According to many residents, some of the

buildings in this town, designated as a UNESCO World Heritage Site, are haunted.

One of the buildings where apparitions are considered to be commonplace is the Boscawen Inn, a Queen Anne style structure built in 1888. Patrons of the inn often find their beds unmade after the maids have cleaned the room. Towels are found on the floor of the bathroom, and maids often do extra checks on each room just to be sure that no ghosts have rumpled the beds.

According to the town historian, Eric Croft, the best-known ghost resides at the Lunenburg Academy, the elementary school in town. The building itself is a combination of High Victorian, French Second Empire, and Queen Anne architectural styles, and as you might expect, a graveyard borders it on two sides.

Different stories are connected with the academy, but a particularly startling one is that a gnarled hand emerges from one of the basement toilets. Children frequently have nightmares about this possibility. One stall in the girl's washroom has a door nailed shut and a sign that reads "Do Not Use!"

Jake and Peter have not seen any ghosts, but they are enjoying the many other wonderful sights.

Friday August 8

Gardens are not made by singing "Oh, how beautiful," and sitting in the shade.

Rudyard Kipling

How true that is! My friend Will has a magnificent garden, but I know of no one who works harder at it than he does. For years following his retirement, he has spent many hours each day hoeing and weeding, clipping and pruning.

Some of Will's friends ask why he works so hard when he could be relaxing or doing other things. Will has his answer ready.

"Work? Being in my garden isn't work. I spent many years working in an office and dreaming of being in my garden. I love every minute here. Being with my plants and flowers is a great joy for me. Anything that I love doing can't be called 'work'."

Saturday August 9

In the month of August I feel so nicely settled into summer.

The days are warm, the evenings are long and starry, and fruits and vegetables taste as they never do in winter.

August days are calming. No one seems hurried, and even when it rains, it does so gently.

I enjoy enjoying August!

Sunday August 10

For flowers that bloom about our feet,
For tender grass so fresh and sweet,
For song of bird and hum of bee,
For all things fair, we hear and see
Father in Heaven we thank Thee!

Ralph Waldo Emerson

Monday August 11

I am so pleased to be back here in Muskoka with my dear friend Eleanor. Each year I look forward with eager anticipation to the time we spend together in this beautiful area of Ontario.

Eleanor's cottage is one of those large old homes that was built at the turn of the century. It has bright, airy bedrooms, a country-sized living room and kitchen and, loveliest of all, an enormous screened-in porch that runs across the entire front of the cottage.

Each morning Eleanor and I enjoy our tea on the porch as we watch for the steamship *Segwun* to pass by. This lovely old ship is a reminder of the gracious way of travelling the lake that existed over a century ago. The youngsters that often follow the *Segwun* on their jet skis bring us quickly back to the present.

I think that Pythagoras may have put it best when he said, "Friendship—one soul in two bodies."

Tuesday August 12

There is a serene and settled majesty to woodland scenery that enters into the soul and delights and elevates it, and fills it with noble inclinations.

Washington Irving

Wednesday August 13

August usually finds us in a daily routine of healthy outdoor activities, which often means that people develop healthy appetites to match. Isn't it lucky that this circumstance coincides with the time of bountiful harvest? Fruits and vegetables are ripening faster than we are able to use them. Luckily, our forbearers developed many ways to preserve our food—drying, smoking, salting, pickling, canning and freezing—many of which are still used at this time of year.

When I was young and newly married, I was anxious to prove that I was an able (and frugal) cook. I decided that I would take some tomatoes, peppers, onions and cabbage that grew so abundantly in our garden and make a piccalilli relish. I worked all day chopping and cooking the vegetables, sterilizing the jars and making what I hoped would be a delicious relish to use all winter long. Unhappily, in my zeal I misread the recipe and instead of adding a 1/4 cup of salt, I added 4 cups of salt. (The fact that this didn't seem wrong at

the time shows the depth of my kitchen inexperi-
ence when I was first married.) I served the relish
at dinner, and to his credit, George really tried to
eat some, but when his mouth puckered and
tears came to his eyes, I knew I had made a mistake of major proportions!

Thursday August 14

When I am attacked by gloomy thoughts,
nothing helps me so much as running to
my books. They quickly absorb me and banish
the clouds from my mind.

M. De Montaigne

Friday August 15

In this hot weather, the many children in cottage country spend countless hours in the
lake. Eleanor's next-door neighbours have three
small children, all of whom are fine swimmers.
In spite of this fact, the parents have wisely chosen to have their children wear life jackets from
the time they get up until the time they go to
bed. As they told me, "Toddlers have drowned
even when several adults have been present but
not paying attention."

Although the children are good swimmers, the
life jacket provides extra protection—and peace
of mind for their parents.

Saturday August 16

Love doesn't make the world go round. Love is what makes the ride worthwhile.

E. P. Jones

Sunday August 17

The Bible is God's chart for you to steer by, to keep you from the bottom of the sea, and to show you where the harbour is, and how to reach it without running on rocks and bars.

Henry Ward Beecher

Monday August 18

I have lived a good many years and have seen things become a part of our everyday lives that were mere dreams when I was a child: dishwashers, microwave ovens, vacuum cleaners, television. The one item that has brought me more pleasure than any of those is the camera.

The camera, once a large, unwieldy item used almost exclusively in a photographer's studio, is now the size of a deck of cards and usable by everyone, even underwater.

Although I have a good memory, time can make fuzzy the mind's images. A photo freezes for all time a wedding day, a baby's first smile, a family picnic.

I have albums of hundreds of photos that include family and dear friends. What a delight to take out these albums and relive the happy times pictured there.

I hope that the pictures I have kept will keep the family memories alive for my grandchildren, and in turn for their grandchildren.

The camera is something I treasure!

Tuesday August 19

Eleanor hosted a lovely dinner party last evening. Eight of us enjoyed a delicious meal and some very interesting discussions.

Our friend Arnold decided to give us a test that the late Charles Schulz had put to his friends. To help put things in proper perspective, Arnold Canadianized the test. You might like to try it too.

—Name the five wealthiest people in the world.

—Name the last five Hart Trophy winners.

—Name the last five winners of the award for most valuable Grey Cup player.

—Name ten people who have won the Nobel or Pulitzer prize.

—Name the last five Prime Ministers of Canada. How did you do?

The point is that few of us remember the headlines of yesterday. A person may be the best in their field, but individual achievements are often forgotten.

Here is another quiz:

—List a few teachers who have influenced your life.

—Name three friends who helped you through a difficult time.

—Name five people who have taught you something worthwhile.

—Think of five people you have enjoyed spending time with.

—Name the three heroes whose stories have inspired you.

This was easier, right?

The point is that the people who make a difference in your life are the ones who care. This is a good thing to remember.

Wednesday August 20

Willpower is the ability, after you have used three-quarters of a can of paint and finished the job, to close the can and clean the brush instead of painting something that doesn't need it.

Thursday August 21

I offer these words of Garnett Ann Schulz to my friend Eleanor with thanks.

To me you are the dearest friend
That I have ever known,
No matter what tomorrow sends
I never feel alone,

As faithful as the rising sun
With peace and joy to lend,
I thank God in my every prayer
For giving me my friend.

Friday August 22

As lovely as it is to be away and enjoy a vacation, it is wonderful to come home again. Will Carleton put it well in these lines:

If there's a heaven upon the earth,
A fellow knows it when
He's been away from home a week,
And then gets back again.

Saturday August 23

The twins have spent the last few days shopping and getting themselves organized to

NASTURTIUM
Tropaeolum

leave for university. There seems to be so much to do, but both Justin and Jenny are well organized and very anxious to begin this wonderful new adventure. I know that Phyllis and Bill are so very proud of their children and pleased that they have chosen to continue their education, but I know, as well, that they will miss the children very much when they are gone.

There are only two lasting bequests that we can give our children. One of these is roots, the other is wings.

Hodding Carter

Sunday August 24

Some years ago while visiting with friends in Vermont, we attended a local church. While leafing through their Book of Common Prayer before the service began, I discovered a beautiful prayer for seniors.

Look with mercy, O God our Father, on all whose increasing years bring them weakness, distress, or isolation. Provide for them homes of dignity and peace; give them understanding helpers, and the willingness to accept help; and as their strength diminishes, increase their faith and their assurance of your love. Amen.

Monday August 25

This last week of August brings to a close the school summer holiday.

Although many of the children may grumble, most of them are pleased to come home from camp or the cottage and to see old friends again.

On my morning walk I noticed a real change in our community. Where there had been quiet the past number of weeks, there was now the happy chatter of children.

Although I regret the end of another beautiful summer, I do enjoy our young neighbours' presence again.

Tuesday August 26

If you want your children to keep their feet on the ground, put some responsibility on their shoulders.

Wednesday August 27

Some years ago, the Kansas City *Star* ran an ad in the personals column that had eight long words—reprehensible, idiosyncrasy, extrapolate, platitudinous, assiduous, plethora, euthanasia, and desiderata. The ad was signed Ronnie Johnson.

The editor wondered what was going on so he sent a reporter to find Ronnie. It turned out that Ronnie was a high school sophomore whose English teacher had told the students that she would give an A to anyone who found those eight words in the paper in the first semester.

Thursday August 28

Our family loves corn! We are always looking for ways to enjoy this delicious vegetable. One of the many ways to serve it is in corn fritters. The first time I ever tried a corn fritter was in Macon, Georgia. George and I were attending a conference in this southern U.S. state, and we were eating in a small diner. We ordered our dinner and, as a side dish, the waitress brought a half dozen of the golden fritters and a jar of syrup. One bite and we were hooked.

Corn Fritters

1 cup fresh sweet corn (canned or frozen may
    be used when corn is out of season.)
1/2 tsp. salt
1/2 cup milk
2 eggs
2 cups flour
2 tsp. baking soda

Mix all of the ingredients into a thick batter and drop by the spoonful into hot fat 1/2" deep. Cook about 3 minutes on each side or until golden in colour. Drain on paper towel. Serve hot with butter and maple syrup.

Friday August 29

Summer is such a fleeting time. The nights grow cooler and the occasional leaf has now begun to take on a golden hue. It seems only yesterday that we watched so carefully for the green shoots and buds and now suddenly we are approaching the time of harvest.

As sad as I am to see summer's end, I look forward to the beauty that is autumn in Canada.

Saturday August 30

Just think how happy you'd be if you lost everything you have right now—and then got it all back again.

Sunday August 31

There were a number of youngsters at our morning service of worship. It was a delight to sing with them one of the loveliest of children's hymns, "Jesus Loves Me."

Jesus loves me! this I know,
For the Bible tells me so;
Little ones to Him belong,
They are weak but He is strong.
Yes, Jesus loves me,
Yes, Jesus loves me,
Yes, Jesus loves me,
The Bible tells me so.

Anna B. Warner

September

Monday September 1

Labour Day

I thank the unknown author for these lines that I feel define the essence of this holiday.

Today is here and mine to use . . .
Tomorrow may not be;
And so the present world I choose
To task my energy.

The opportunity I hold
Within my hand today
May prove to be the precious mould
To shape my future way.

Today is still the only time
In which to do my work,
And mighty triumphs, deeds sublime,
May in its moments lurk.

And even though the lowly vale
Of common life is my way,
The only thing that will avail
Is duty done today.

Tuesday September 2

In our area, this is the first day of school. I have such respect for the teachers and the difficult job that is theirs. Phyllis' friend Christie, a teacher, provided this story for today. I hope you find it as amusing as I did.

"Survivor" is a very popular television show. A number of educators suggested this format for a new survivor show.

Three businessmen and three businesswomen will be placed in an elementary school for 6 weeks.

Each businessperson will be provided with a copy of the school district's curriculum and a class of students.

Each class will have five learning-disabled children, three with attention deficit disorder, one gifted child and two who speak limited English. Three will be labeled as having "severe behaviour problems."

Lesson plans must be completed three days in advance, with annotations for curriculum objectives. Contestants must modify, organize or create materials accordingly.

The business people will be required to teach students, handle misconduct, implement technology, correct homework, make bulletin boards, compute grades, write report cards, communicate with parents and arrange parent conferences.

They will supervise recess and monitor hall-ways. They must attend workshops. They must tutor those students who are behind.

Lunch is limited to 30 minutes, and the restroom will be available to them only if another staff member is available to supervise their class.

The businesspeople will advance their education on their own time and pay for this training themselves. (This can be accomplished by moonlighting at a second job or marrying someone with money).

The winner will be allowed to return to his or her job. The others are required to stay in teaching.

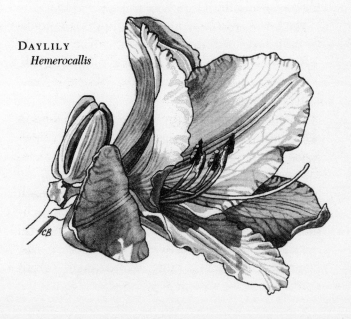

DAYLILY
Hemerocallis

Wednesday September 3

No race can prosper till it learns that there is as much dignity in tilling a field as in writing a poem.

Booker T. Washington

Thursday September 4

The fellow who worries about what people think of him wouldn't worry so much if he only knew how seldom they do.

Friday September 5

Season of mists and yellow fruitfulness!
Close bosom friend of the maturing sun;
Conspiring with him how to lead and bless
With fruit the vines that round the thatch-
   eves run.

John Keats

Saturday September 6

It's said that success in marriage is more than finding the right person; it's being the right person.

How true! At a time when divorce and family breakup is becoming more and more prevalent, both partners in a marriage must work hard if that marriage is to be successful.

The temptation is great to lay the blame for problems on someone else. Both partners must make every effort to be the best that they can be for themselves and for their spouse.

Being the right person isn't easy, but it certainly is worth every bit of effort that is put into it.

Sunday September 7

The saying of grace before each meal has always been a part of my life. Of the many ways of giving thanks, one of my favourites is one that the young children in our family like to sing at this time of year, the "Johnny Appleseed" grace.

"Oh, the Lord is good to me, and so I thank the Lord for giving me the things I need, the sun and the rain and the appleseed. The Lord is good to me!"

Monday September 8

Marg and I volunteer at our local elementary school. Most often we help with the reading program, but occasionally we get involved with the school plays or talent presentations.

One of the few problems with such presentations is that some of the younger children are often disappointed if they are not selected for a particular role in the play for which they tried out.

On this afternoon, Billy, who had not been awarded the role he coveted, was very excited to tell me, "Mrs. McCann, guess what! I don't get to be the 'Big Bad Wolf,' but I was chosen to clap and cheer."

Billy's teacher is a very tactful person.

Tuesday September 9

One of the largest lessons we have to learn in this life, and one that many persons never learn, is to see the divine, the celestial, the pure in the common—the near at hand. To see that heaven lies about us here in the world.

John Burrows

Wednesday September 10

Marg, Bruce and I attended a friend's birthday party this evening. John, one of the other guests, had a great deal of information about the origin of the birthday party. I hope you find this as interesting as I did.

The first birthday parties were reserved for royalty because no records were kept of the birth dates of the commoners. One of the first birthdays recorded—Pharaoh's—is described in the book of Genesis. It featured a great household feast with servants and family members invited.

The Greeks were among the first to keep birth records for everyone, but only the heads of important families celebrated the special day.

By the twelfth century, Christians, who kept birth records of their children and often named them after a saint, usually celebrated on the saint's feast day as well as the actual birthday.

To the ancient Greeks, birthday candles had special magic for granting wishes. This is why we make a wish before blowing out the candles.

Although we usually enjoy a cake for our birthday, Russians often have pie, and Icelanders indulge with canned fruit. Danes hang a flag out the window on a birthday.

The party this evening was a celebration fit for a king!

Thursday September 11

On September 11, 2001, as the world watched in horror, there was an unprecedented terrorist attack on the United States of America. Airplanes crashed, buildings crumbled and many thousands of people lost their lives.

Those of us who followed the events on television wept for people we didn't know. Many gave blood in hope that lives would be saved, and many more donated money, hoping somehow to lessen the sorrow of the thousands of people who lost family members in this unforgettable tragedy.

Rudolph Giuliani, mayor of New York City, said at the time, "New York City will never be the same after September 11. It will be better."

We hope that this can be said for us all: our world will never be the same; it will be better.

Friday September 12

On my walk through the neighbourhood today, I was surprised to see how many leaves have changed colour. The big old maple tree on the corner is a stunning crimson shade, and several of the trees at the millpond have turned a beautiful bright yellow. I was reminded of these lines:

> The flaming hills of autumn
> Are a wonder to behold,
> When all the countryside
> Turns to red and gold.

Saturday September 13

The goal of science is to describe the universe; the goal of religion is to find the most abundant life which man may possess in such a universe.

Kirtley F. Mather

Sunday September 14

Abide with us, O Lord, for it is toward evening and the day is far spent; abide with us and with the whole church. Abide with us in the evening of the day, in the evening of life, in the evening of this world. Abide with us and with all the faithful ones, O Lord, in time and in eternity.

Lutheran Manual of Prayer

Monday September 15

When my friends and I get together, our discussions often turn to our grandchildren. Most of us at one time or another have taken a turn at babysitting our grandchildren, and on occasion it turns out to be more than we bargained for.

My friends Betty and John were taking care of their two youngest grandchildren, ages four and two, while their son and daughter-in-law attended a convention in British Columbia.

As John related, "Everything seemed to be going well—and then their parents left."

"Edna, I don't believe that they had been gone more than an hour when Marissa accidentally knocked over a large glass of grape juice on her bedroom carpet. In spite of our best efforts, the carpet retained the bright purple stain.

"In the meantime, Jacob awoke from his nap covered in a rash that (after a rushed trip to the doctor) turned out to be an allergic reaction to the medication he was taking for a bronchial infection.

"Over the rest of the week, Marissa picked up the same infection, and neither child ever slept more than two hours at a time.

"Edna, I love those two youngsters with my heart and soul, but I have never been happier to see my son and his wife arrive home.

"We are still recovering!"

"A mother is one who can take the place of all others, but whose place no one can take."

Tuesday September 16

This is the time of year when baseball season is winding down and the playoffs are on the horizon. I have been a fan of the Toronto Blue Jays for many years, and I follow the games on both radio and television. I know that my husband, George, would be quite surprised to know what a fan I have become because, on many occasions years ago, I told George that watching baseball was akin to watching the grass grow.

I often invite friends over to enjoy a game on television, and I like to serve my own version of Cracker Jacks. This recipe is easy and delicious.

Popcorn Syrup for Caramel Nut Popcorn

1/2 cup sugar
1/2 cup dark corn syrup
1/2 tsp. salt

Combine sugar, corn syrup and salt. When popcorn is popped, reduce heat to medium, and pour the syrup over the popcorn. Mix in 1 cup salted peanuts. Stir for 2 to 3 minutes to coat the popcorn and nuts well, then turn out onto a large sheet of foil. Spread evenly and let stand to allow the syrup to harden a bit. Let cool thoroughly and serve in bowls to your fellow fans.

Wednesday September 17

Elsie Grant gives us these lines for today as we head toward autumn.

As Summer Leaves

In autumn, breezes cool
Mark the end of summer's rule. . .
Fragrant mow and laden bin,
Prove the harvest's gathered in.

Shorter day and longer night,
Winging birds in homeward flight,
Haze of blue the woods enfold,
Falling maples red and gold.

In autumn, colour flares
From the bounty nature spares . . .
Richer, brighter still it glows
Than midsummer ever shows.

And the crickets mournfully
Sing of winter soon to be . . .
Light the lamp and close the door,
Summer's gone its way once more.

Thursday September 18

The highest compliment one person can bestow on another is to ask for advice.

Friday September 19

Cheerfulness and contentment are great beautifiers and are famous preservers of youthful looks.

Charles Dickens

Saturday September 20

Jenny and Justin called today, and we had a wonderful conversation about their first few weeks of university. Both seem to be making a good adjustment to life away from home and to the rigors of higher education.

Much of the credit for this, I believe, should go to Phyllis and Bill, who always encouraged their children to set high standards for themselves and gave them endless encouragement as they worked toward their goals.

A wise parent knows that the more a child feels valued, the better his or her values will be. Phyllis and Bill are such parents.

Sunday September 21

Ring ye bells of joy and praise;
Ring throughout the harvest days;
Ring across the golden fields,
Praise where earth her bounty yields.

Rev. J. E. Ward

Monday September 22

Today we welcome our most beautiful season of the year, autumn. Probably nothing can make the coming of winter more acceptable than the sight of the trees aflame in the autumn sunlight. It is almost as if Nature feels obliged to give us this magical beauty to carry us through the gray days to come.

Tuesday September 23

I'm not sure of the original source of these lines, but the poem was sent to me by Laura and Robert, elderly friends of mine living in Alberta.

Age is a state of mind . . .
If you've left your dreams behind,
If hope is lost; if you no longer look ahead,
If your ambitious fires are dead—
Then you are old!
But if in life you hold the best
And if in life you keep the zest,
If love of God and man you hold
No matter how the years go by . . .
No matter how the birthdays fly—
You are not old!

Wednesday September 24

The sun, with all those planets moving around it, can ripen the smallest bunch of grapes as

INDIAN SUMMER

if it had nothing else to do. Why then should I doubt His power?

Galileo

Thursday September 25

A British hostess dealt with boring dinner companions in an unusual way. She would say to them, "My dear, what you are telling me is so interesting, you must go away and write it down."

Friday September 26

Henry Wadsworth Longfellow once said, "Music is the universal language of mankind."

Music was always an important part of our family life, and over the years I have come to appreciate music of all types—from the music of the church to jazz, classical and even rock-and-roll.

I offer today these thoughts about music:

Those who are not touched by music, I hold to be like sticks and stones.

Martin Luther

Music to the mind is as air to the body.

Plato

Music is a revelation; a revelation loftier than all wisdom and all philosophy.

Ludwig von Beethoven

Where words fail, music speaks.

Hans Christian Andersen

All art constantly aspires towards the condition of music.

Walter Pater

When I hear music I fear no danger, I am invulnerable, I see no foe. I am related to the earliest times and to the latest.

Henry David Thoreau

Saturday September 27

It is the Indian Summer. The rising sun blazes through the misty air like a conflagration. A yellowish smoky haze fills the atmosphere, and a filmy mist lies like a silver lining on the sky. The wind is soft and low. It wafts to us the odour of forest leaves that hang wilted on the dripping branches, or drop into the stream. Their gorgeous tints are gone, as if the autumnal rains have washed them out. Orange, yellow and scarlet are all changed to one melancholy russet hue.

The birds, too, have taken wing, and have left their roofless dwellings. Not the whistle of a robin, not the twitter of an eavesdropping swallow, not the carol of one sweet, familiar voice. All gone. Only the dismal cawing of a crow, as he sits and curses that the harvest is over; or the chit-chat of an idle squirrel, the noisy denizen of a hollow tree, the mendicant friar of a large parish, the absolute monarch of a dozen acorns.

Longfellow

Sunday September 28

Fear thou not; for I am with thee: be not dismayed; for I am thy God: I will strengthen thee; yea, I will help thee; yea, I will uphold thee with the right hand of my righteousness.

Isaiah 41:10

Monday September 29

My grandson Marshall, a lawyer, made me laugh with this story today.

A criminal case in court was coming to an end. All witnesses had been heard, and both lawyers had made final presentations.

The accused, given a chance to speak on his own behalf, made an impassioned plea to the judge, ending with, "As God is my judge, I'm completely innocent."

The judge replied, "I'm not . . . you aren't . . . two years!"

Tuesday September 30

A problem for many of us seniors is getting enough exercise to stay fit and healthy.

As the time passes, our physical strength diminishes, and staying active becomes more of a challenge.

I have found, and my doctor agrees, that walking is probably the easiest and safest way to keep fit.

Several short walks a day, even in poor weather, are a wonderful benefit to young and old alike.

When I am walking I seem to think more clearly, and a walk on a good day seems to lift my spirits as little else does.

My doctor and I heartily recommend this excellent exercise. It is even more enjoyable when it is done with a friend.

October

Falling Leaves

What are the things I love to see
In autumn when the year grows old?
The black gum leaves of scarlet red;
A hillside poplar turned to gold.

What are the things I love to hear
In autumn when the year is spent?
The wild geese flying overhead,
And drowsy rain with its clean scent.

What are the things I love to smell
In autumn when the year is done?
Blue curling smoke from burning leaves,
And wild grapes purpling in the sun.

Ah, autumn in her passing leaves
The memory of a lonely song,
And for the heart a legacy
That will last all winter long.

William Arnette Wooford

Thursday October 2

Faith is the soul's insight or discovery of some reality that enables a man to stand anything that can happen to him in the universe.

Josiah Royce

Friday October 3

My son-in-law Bruce wages an ongoing "battle of the bulge." He loves to eat and he enjoys his food so much that keeping his weight in check is often a struggle. Jake Frampton was telling Bruce tonight that Julia Child (America's first television chef) had an answer for truly desperate dieters.

When Ms. Child was in college, her nickname was "skinny." However, over the years of testing recipes for her show and books, her weight began to creep upward. Tempted by such things as raw pastry dough, chocolate, mayonnaise and many other high calorie items in her recipes, she decided that she needed a 1200 calorie-a-day diet.

On this diet she managed to stick to tea, fruit and an egg for breakfast; vegetables and cottage cheese for lunch, and for dinner, lamb, corn (no butter) an apple and one glass of red wine. She walked half an hour a day and, when truly tempted, offered this advice, "Take a bite, chew it—and spit it out!"

Saturday October 4

To reach the port of heaven we must sail, sometimes with the wind and sometimes against it—but we must sail, not drift or lie at anchor.

Oliver Wendell Holmes

Sunday October 5

Every good gift and every perfect gift is from above, and cometh down from the Father.

James 1:17

Monday October 6

As Marg and I walked through the fallen leaves today, I was reminded of how much I love this beautiful season. Many years ago, Mary and her husband John were a very long way from home and missing the colours of autumn enormously.

Mary sounded so homesick that George and I decided to do something to help. We went outdoors and collected as many brightly coloured leaves as we could and put them in a large box. We had leaves of all kinds—maple, oak, beech, birch, aspen—in a multitude of colours.

We sealed the box and mailed it to Mary. She was delighted. "I waxed some," she wrote, "and then I put the rest in the kitchen where I could see them whenever I wanted. When they were so dry they became brittle, I sprinkled them in our fireplace whenever we had a fire. It was a wonderful smell of home!"

Tuesday October 7

My daughter Julia remarked to me today that she seems to be involved in so many things that she has very little time for herself.

Often the desire to be well thought of makes us reluctant to say no to anyone who requests our time. We look on requests for our time or abilities as a compliment for the things we do well.

If we don't cultivate our ability to say no to activities for which we have no real time or interest, then we'll miss opportunities to say yes to the things that matter most to us.

Julia has always been a most cheerful and willing assistant, so people enjoy calling upon her time and time again. Without realizing it, she found herself involved in more things than she could handle.

The difficult thing now, of course, is deciding how to extricate herself from at least some of these commitments. I gave what I hope is some good advice.

"Explain to the people what happened and that you are unable to fulfill these obligations. I'm sure that they will understand and respect your honesty. Better that they find someone who is able to do the job well."

Wednesday October 8

> Autumn with its clear, crisp air
> and sunsets of coppery hue,
> Has gently pushed away summer
> to linger till winter is due.
>
> *Author unknown*

Thursday October 9

Apples are a delightful treat in the fall, and this recipe for Apple Pandowdy is one of our favourites to use for the coming Thanksgiving dinner.

Apple Pandowdy

2 tbsp. + 1/4 cup butter, divided

8 apples (about 3 lbs.), preferably Golden Delicious, peeled, cored, and cut into 8 slices per apple

1/2 cup molasses

2 tbsp. + 1 1/2 cups all-purpose flour, divided

2 tbsp. lemon juice

2 tbsp. ground cinnamon

2 tsp. vanilla extract, divided in two

1/2 tsp. ground nutmeg

1/2 cup + 3 tbsp. sugar, divided

1 tsp. baking powder

1/2 tsp. salt

2 eggs

1/2 cup milk

1/2 pint sweetened whipped cream

Preheat oven to 350° F. Butter a 6-cup oval baking dish. Cut 2 tbsp. butter into small pieces; set aside. In a large bowl combine apples, molasses, lemon juice, 2 tbsp. flour, cinnamon, 1 tsp. vanilla extract and nutmeg. Let stand 15 minutes. Arrange mixture evenly in baking dish; dot with reserved butter. Set aside.

Melt remaining butter; cool slightly. Combine 1/2 cup sugar, baking powder, salt and remaining flour. In a bowl, beat together eggs, milk, melted butter and remaining vanilla. Stir milk mixture into the flour mixture until the ingredients are just combined. (Batter will be very thick.)

Spoon batter over apple mixture, spreading as needed to cover apples and allowing batter to pour down between apples. Sprinkle batter with remaining sugar. Bake 40 to 45 minutes or until crust is golden and filling is bubbly. Serve warm with whipped cream.

Makes 8 servings.

Friday October 10

The way I see it, if you want the rainbow, you've got to put up with the rain.

Dolly Parton

Saturday October 11

With the football season in full swing again, I enjoyed our neighbour's story.

He was watching the game on television and,

in the heat of the action, commented to no one in particular:

"That quarterback is hopeless! He hasn't hit one receiver all day and he's fumbled twice. Why don't they take him out of the game?"

With a logic that can only come from a child, his son said, "It's probably his ball, dad."

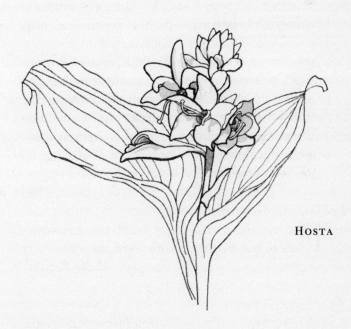

HOSTA

Sunday October 12

And now, on this our festal day,
Thy bounteous hand confessing,
Upon thine altar, Lord, we lay
The first fruits of thy blessing:
By thee the souls of men are fed
With gifts of grace supernal;
Thou who dost give us daily bread,
Give us the bread eternal.

William Chatterton Dix

Monday October 13

Thanksgiving Day

We have so much to be grateful for today. Our family has always made Thanksgiving a time for reunion, and this year was no exception. We all put a great deal of effort into the occasion, and I am delighted to renew our family ties and the bonds of love that keep our family close.

My grandson Mickey read this prayer from Robert Louis Stevenson before our meal.

Lord, behold our family here assembled. We thank Thee for this place in which we dwell; for the love that unites us; for the peace accorded us this day; for the hope with which we expect tomorrow; for the health, the work, the food and the bright skies that make our lives delightful; for our friends in all parts of the earth, and our friendly helpers.

Tuesday October 14

The making of friends who are real friends is the token we have of a man's success in life.

Edward Everett Hale

Wednesday October 15

"We never really comprehend death until it takes someone we love." This statement has a great impact for those of us who are older and have lost many of our friends and loved ones. Fortunately for those of us who have a great faith in eternal life, the "comprehension of death" is also the belief and understanding of our life to come.

Thursday October 16

Earlier this week our friends in the U.S. celebrated Columbus Day. On October 12, in 1492, Christopher Columbus discovered America. It took a man with tenacity and unflinching devotion to a single idea to confront the perils that he faced in his attempt to reach land to the west.

He accomplished more than anyone else towards making us masters of the world we tread, and giving us, instead of yawning abysses and realms of vapour, wide waters for our ships, and land for the city and the plough. . . . He stands in history as the completer of the globe.

John Sterling

Friday October 17

It can be very tough for the young people to understand that there are difficulties to be faced in aging.

Some years ago, Phyllis had a friend who taught at a local college. He was explaining to his students that many elderly people have hearing loss, problems with eyesight and so on. The students wrote accurate notes of the information given, but the teacher felt that they couldn't really appreciate these problems without first-hand knowledge.

In order to help them understand, he devised an ingenious plan. The students were paired off for the day. In the morning one of the students was given a pair of eyeglasses to wear that had a thin coating of Vaseline smeared on them. They had to put cotton in their ears and several pebbles in their shoes. The "seeing" partner then took the "aging" student somewhere in the community and stayed with them as they tried to find their way back to the college. In the afternoon, the roles were reversed.

Many of the students were near to tears of frustration before they were able to return to the college. This practical demonstration gave the students a tremendous insight that no amount of lecturing could ever accomplish.

"Old age is like everything else; to make a success of it, you've got to start young."

SUNFLOWER
Helianthus

Saturday October 18

I wonder how many of my readers are old enough to remember eating buckwheat pancakes that were made from scratch. I had almost forgotten about them until Marg made us a pancake breakfast using a very popular boxed mix with the instructions "just add water and one egg."

Perhaps it was because we made these pancakes on the coldest of winter mornings that I have such fond memories of their good taste. Whatever the reason, let me take you back and see if it makes your mouth water too.

We would start the batter several days before we planned to have the pancakes. We had a heavy old pitcher, and we'd begin with a pinch of salt in two cups of warm water; we added a yeast cake along with two tablespoons of brown sugar and about 1 cup of white flour and 2 cups of buckwheat flour. This would be mixed together and allowed to rise in a cool place until the next night. The mixture would be bubbling by now, and to this we would add more water and white and buckwheat flour until we had a batter that would pour easily. This was left overnight—usually in the fruit cellar—and by morning we were ready to go.

George would take our heavy iron skillet and grease it with a piece of salt pork before pouring the batter into good-sized rounds. Flipped once and then served on a plate with bacon and maple syrup, this was a breakfast to remember!

Is your mouth watering yet?

Sunday October 19

The souls of the righteous are in the hand of God, and there shall no torment touch them.

The Apocrypha

Monday October 20

Tomorrow's fate, though thou be wise,
Thou canst not tell nor yet surmise;

Pass therefore not today in vain,
For it will never come again.

Omar Khayyam

Tuesday October 21

Each of us has our own idea of success. Often young people feel that success is based on how much you earn or what you own. My mother never attended university, nor did she become wealthy, but she was a success at living, which is the greatest success of all.

Of course there is no formula for success, except perhaps an unconditional acceptance of life and what it brings.

Arthur Rubenstein

Wednesday October 22

This time of year gives us a wonderful opportunity to decorate our homes. Marg and I spent this afternoon making some very special floral arrangements. They are a simple but effective way to bring some of autumn's beauty indoors. If you would like to make one of these arrangements, you'll need:

—A clear mason jar
—Enough cranberries (fresh or frozen) to almost fill the jar
—Hardy mums in your favourite fall colours, cut from the garden or purchased

MORNING GLORY
Ipomoea

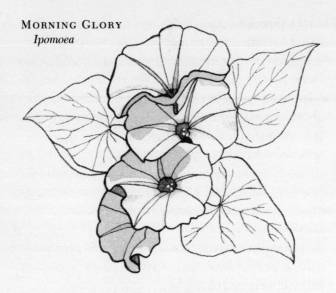

—Small bunch of dried wheat
—Several pine branches
—Coloured leaves (maple, oak etc.)
—Length of cranberry-coloured ribbon

Fill the jar almost full with cranberries. Add water to the top of the jar. Arrange the mums and the pine branches in the jar. Add the wheat and coloured leaves. Use the ribbon to tie around the jar in a bow.

This makes a most attractive gift to give at this time of year. Add water to the jar as needed.

Thursday October 23

The really happy man is the one who can enjoy the scenery when he has to take a detour.

Friday October 24

My sister Sarah and her husband Richard live on Canada's east coast. As children we lived on the coast of Nova Scotia, and although Sarah has been in other parts of the country for short periods of time, she always returns to the province that she knows and loves.

Sarah and I have talked about this often.

"You know, Edna," Sarah will say, "You and I are very different. You adapt so well and enjoy yourself wherever you are, while I really only feel comfortable when I am in Nova Scotia. As much as I wish that I lived closer to you, the thought of Richard and I leaving this area that we know and love so well makes my heart literally ache."

I know that Sarah is not alone in this feeling. Many people find one place in this world that suits them, and living elsewhere is simply unthinkable.

My brother Ben and I often used to tease Sarah about this until we realized how much her province means to her. Sarah gets so much pleasure from knowing everyone in her small town, from seeing "her" ocean every day, and from the sights and smells that are part of her life there that she would indeed be foolish to leave Nova Scotia.

There is nothing like staying at home for real comfort.

Jane Austen

READY FOR
HALLOWEEN

Saturday October 25

Conscience may not prevent you from doing wrong, but it sure will keep you from enjoying it.

Sunday October 26

The Lord bless thee, and keep thee: The Lord make his face shine upon thee and be gracious unto thee: The Lord lift up his countenance upon thee, and give thee peace.

Numbers 6:24–26

Monday October 27

I was having trouble sleeping last night, so I turned on my television. I enjoyed seeing a very old Charlie Chaplin film and I laughed out loud as I remembered a story that my friend Mavis told me some years ago.

When Chaplin was at the peak of his popularity, a theatre held a Charlie Chaplin–look-alike contest. The winner would receive a silver cup. Chaplin, without telling anyone, decided to enter the contest himself. He came second.

Tuesday October 28

I like this wise advice: treasure your children for what they are, not for what you want them to be.

Wednesday October 29

Mark Twain's words have meaning for many of us oldsters.

"It isn't so astonishing the number of things I can remember as the number of things I can remember that aren't so."

Thursday October 30

We are always complaining our days are few and acting as though there would be no end of them.

Friday October 31

I wish that you could be with us
On Hallowe'en at night;
We'd light a lot of candles,
And they would shine so bright
That all the little Brownies
And Goblins roundabout,
Would come and dance upon our lawn
And sing and play and shout.

Author unknown

November

Saturday November 1

No warmth nor cheer nor ease,
No comfortable feel in any member,
No shade, no shine, no butterflies, no bees,
No fruits, no flowers, no leaves, no birds
No—vember

This is the way Englishman Thomas Hood saw
November, and many of us feel the same way
about this grey and dreary month. The first day
of November does give us a reason to rejoice.
This is All Saints Day, a day to pause and give
thanks for all those good people who make our
lives a little bit better.

Give us grace so to follow your blessed Saints in
all virtuous and godly living, that we may come
to those ineffable joys that you have prepared for
those who truly love you; through Jesus Christ
our Lord. Amen.

Book of Common Prayer

Sunday November 2

O heavenly Father, who hast filled the world
with beauty: Open our eyes to behold thy

gracious hand in all thy works; that, rejoicing in thy whole creation, we may learn to serve thee with gladness.

Book of Common Prayer

Monday November 3

My great-granddaughter, Bethany, continues to enjoy her gymnastics class very much. This past weekend I had a chance to attend one of her competitions. I was amazed by the level of expertise that these young athletes displayed.

Bethany, who is eleven years old now, competes in a series of events, and she and her team mates were very successful, each earning a number of medals.

Although the team was excited and proud of themselves, they and the coach were particularly pleased for one of the competitors on a rival team. This young lady had been injured in a car accident, and this was her first competition since her recovery. When she finished her floor exercise, all of the competitors stood and cheered. Many of us in the audience had tears in our eyes. How nice to see that good sportsmanship is still an important part of youngsters' competition.

Tuesday November 4

"The common cold, when it is treated with decongestants, fluids and bed rest, will clear up in two weeks. Left completely alone, it should be gone in about 14 days."

Whenever I get sick, many of my mother's tried, tested and true remedies come to mind. Beef tea, mutton broth and arrowroot milk porridge are a few of Mother's popular cures. However, the favourite, given to us when we had a cold or the flu or any other malaise, was oatmeal gruel. My, how I hated it! I believe the curative power of gruel lay in the fact that you wanted to feel better just so that you wouldn't need another dose of the ghastly stuff.

"Not feeling well, pet? Perhaps a nice cup of gruel . . ." was threat enough to make me feel better immediately.

This evening I went to bed early and thought about mother's gruel. I believe that I feel better already!

Oatmeal Gruel

Pour 4 tbsp. of the best oatmeal, coarsely ground, into 2 cups of boiling water. Let it boil gently and stir often until it thickens. Strain it and then add to the broth some butter and nutmeg and salt to taste. The sicker the patient, the thinner should be the gruel.

Wednesday November 5

The children in our community frequently ask Marg, Bruce and I to sponsor them in all manner of fundraising efforts. Swim-a-thons, bike-a-thons, skate-a-thons are very popular ways to raise money for schools or charities.

One of the "a-thons" that we have supported for many years is a read-a-thon to raise money for research into multiple sclerosis, a debilitating disease that affects young and old alike.

Our young neighbours read as many books as they can in one month so it is of great benefit to them as well as to the many thousands who suffer from this terrible disease. It feels good to sponsor these youngsters in such a worthwhile cause.

Thursday November 6

Although I handle most things with good humour, there are times when I don't deal with things in my usual way.

I have been down with the flu and a cold and have spent my last few days in bed, blowing my nose, drinking orange juice and eating chicken soup. I have been miserable and cranky and absolutely no fun to be around!

Finally, today I have been feeling somewhat better and, hopefully, my good nature will return soon. I miss it greatly!

Friday November 7

I feel that I'm not alone when I say that I think November is the least attractive month of the year.

The beauty of summer flowers and autumn leaves are gone, but we don't yet have crisp white snow to take their place. Instead we have a dull gray sky, fields of brown stubble, bare trees and a landscape that offers no bright or cheery colours.

My favourite escape from these dismal scenes is a seat in front of a cozy fireplace, a good book and quiet music. Add to this some candles burning and a good hot cup of tea, and suddenly November seems to be much less dreary.

Saturday November 8

When anyone tells you he has no time to read, you can be sure that he is lacking something vital in his life. It would make as much sense as saying, "I have no time to eat."

Sunday November 9

On this Sunday before Remembrance Day, these lines seem so fitting.

O God of Love, O King of Peace,
Make wars throughout the world to cease,
The wrath of sinful man restrain,
Give peace, O God, give peace again.
Rev. Sir H. W. Baker

Monday November 10

Great people are not affected by each puff of wind that blows ill. Like great ships, they sail serenely on, in a calm sea or a great tempest.

Tuesday November 11

Remembrance Day

Lord, make us instruments of your peace.
Where there is hatred, let us sow love.
Where there is injury, pardon.
Where there is discord, union.
Where there is doubt, faith.
Where there is darkness, light.
Divine Master, grant that we may not so
  much seek to be consoled, as to console, to
  be understood, as to understand, to be
  loved, as to love.
For it is in giving that we receive, it is in par-
  doning that we are pardoned, and it is in
  dying that we are born to eternal life.

St. Francis of Assisi

Today we remember with grateful thanks all those men and women who laid down their lives so that we may live in freedom.

Wednesday November 12

Although modern medicine has given us a pill for almost everything, there are still those who believe in the curative powers of many foods. I have kept a list of various fruits and vegetables and the disease or illness that each may help. I thought you might enjoy seeing these old-time cure-alls.

Celery—for any form of rheumatism and nervous dyspepsia.

Lettuce—for insomnia

Onions—for insomnia, coughs and colds, an improved complexion

Carrots—for asthma

Eggs—for hoarseness (beaten egg white, sugar and lemon juice)

Cranberries—for headache, or a fine tonic (eaten raw)

Sour oranges—for rheumatism.

Lemons—for feverish thirst, biliousness, low grade fevers, rheumatism, colds, coughs and liver complaints.

Peanuts—for indigestion.

Thursday November 13

Many great things are accomplished in the face of adversity. Did you know that Mozart, one of the great music composers of all time, was unable to afford heat in his room? Some of his most immortal music was written while his hands were wrapped in woolen socks for warmth.

Friday November 14

November is a wonderful month in which to entertain. I rarely have a large gathering, but I still enjoy having close friends for dinner and an evening of bridge. One of our favourite meals is spaghetti and meatballs. Served with a salad and hot bread it's a delicious way to enjoy a cold November evening.

Spaghetti and Meatballs
Sauce

1 – 28 oz. can tomatoes
1 – 12 oz. can tomato paste
1/2 cup chopped green pepper
3 cloves garlic
4 tbsp. Italian seasoning
1 tsp. salt
1 tsp. pepper
2 cups water

Place all ingredients (except water) in a blender. Blend until smooth. Transfer to a large saucepan, add water and stir.

Meatballs

1 lb. ground beef
3/4 lb ground pork or veal
1/2 cup finely chopped green pepper
1 egg
1/2 cup breadcrumbs

1 tsp. salt
1 tsp. pepper

Combine all ingredients and form into 2-inch balls. Brown meatballs in 2 tsp. oil in a frying pan or place meatballs on a flat oven pan and brown at 350° F. (about 10 minutes). Add meatballs to the spaghetti sauce. Cover and allow the sauce to simmer at least 2 hours. (We often simmer for 6 to 7 hours.) If a thicker sauce is desired, remove lid for approximately 1 hour to allow sauce to thicken.

Saturday November 15

People who have close friends are healthier and happier than those who have none. A single real friend is a treasure worth more than gold or precious stones. Money can buy many things, good and evil. All the wealth in the world could not buy you a friend or pay you for the loss of one.

C. D. Prentice

Sunday November 16

This prayer was translated into English by Chief Yellow Lark of the Sioux Tribe in 1887.

O, Great Spirit whose voice I hear in the wind
Whose breath gives life to the world, hear
   me . . .

I come to you as one of your many children.
I am small and weak.
I need your strength and your wisdom.
May I walk in beauty.
Make my eyes ever behold the red and
    purple sunset.
Make my hands respect the things you have
    made,
And my ears sharp to hear your voice.
Make me wise so that I may know the things
    you have taught your children,
The lessons you have written on every leaf
    and rock.
Make me strong,
Not to be superior to my brothers,
But to fight my greatest enemy—myself.
Make me ever ready to come to you with
    straight eyes
So that when life fades as the fading sunset,
My spirit may come to you without shame.

Monday November 17

I have studied the lives of great men and famous women; and I have found that the men and women who got to the top were those who did the jobs they had in hand, with everything they had of energy and enthusiasm and hard work.

Harry S. Truman

Tuesday November 18

When you encounter difficulties and contradictions, do not try to break them, but bend them with gentleness and time.

Saint Francis de Sales

Wednesday November 19

Age is opportunity no less
Than youth itself, though in another dress.
And as the evening twilight fades away,
The sky is filled with stars invisible by day.

Henry Wadsworth Longfellow

Thursday November 20

Tremendous advances have been made in the field of medicine, and for many doctors organ transplant operations have become almost routine. Some of us may forget just how dramatically an organ transplant can change the life of the recipient and what a wonderful gift is given when organs are donated.

Some time ago I read a thank-you note from a recipient of a heart transplant. It read in part, "I am a heart transplant recipient. Eighteen months after surgery I am forty-one years old, healthy, happy and leading a normal life. It is like a miracle. I feel so blessed.

"I owe this life to someone I have never met, some healthy young person who died unexpectedly. I will be eternally thankful to the family who allowed their loved one's heart to be donated.

"My message is to that unknown family. There is no way I can adequately thank you. I think of you every night, and I shall do so for the rest of my life."

No one of us imagines that we shall die at an early age. How wonderful it is that families give others the gift of life when the lives of their loved ones are tragically cut short.

No one may forsake his neighbour when he is in trouble. Everybody is under obligation to help and support his neighbour as he would himself like to be helped.

Martin Luther

Friday November 21

The past is a source of knowledge and the future is a source of hope. Love of the past implies faith in the future.

Stephen Ambrose

Saturday November 22

The longer I live, the more beautiful life becomes. The earth's beauty grows on man. If you foolishly ignore beauty, you'll find yourself without it. Your life will be impoverished. But if you wisely invest in beauty, it will remain with you all the days of your life.

Frank Lloyd Wright

Sunday November 23

Whatsoever things are true, whatsoever things are honest, whatsoever things are just, whatsoever things are pure, whatsoever things are lovely, whatsoever things are of good report; if there be any virtue, and if there be any praise, think on these things.

Philippians 4:8

Monday November 24

A lovely song, a good book to read,
A letter from a friend,
A cozy room where loved ones are
Safely gathered at day's end . . .
Such pleasant, kind and lovely things
Are of each day a part.
We thank Thee, Lord, that simple things
Light candles in the heart.
For candles lighted in the heart
Can cope with fear and doubt . . .
The lights of beauty, faith and love,
No darkness can snuff out!

Author unknown

Tuesday November 25

My friend Lucy is a nervous flyer. Nevertheless she recently flew to Winnipeg to see her new granddaughter. According to Lucy, the flight out was delightful . . . good weather, a nice meal, pleasant flight attendants.

On the way home, however, severe turbulence and a bumpy landing left many of the passengers somewhat rattled.

A passenger who was leaving the plane just ahead of Lucy addressed the crew as she passed them.

"Did we land," she asked, "or were we shot down?"

Wednesday November 26

My grandson Marshall has his own idea of what makes a good after-dinner speaker: the one who knows all the advantages of stopping sooner than the audience expects.

Thursday November 27

Our American friends are celebrating Thanksgiving Day today. Our family once had a very special Thanksgiving Day in New York City. George had a conference to attend and Marg, Mary, Julia and I tagged along. The conference itself lasted three days so the girls and I had a chance to do some sight-seeing on our own. Our plan was to take the subway to a particular museum of interest, but somehow in the dark of the stations we became confused and lost.

We exited the station and, not knowing where we were, followed a well-dressed woman into a nearby building.

As we entered the building, a very pleasant

man greeted us. "Thank heaven! Four more helpers."

As it turned out, we were in the neighbourhood soup kitchen, and many volunteers were working hard to prepare a traditional turkey dinner for the less fortunate.

After a quick call to let George know where we were, we set about helping wherever we could. The girls set the tables, I made gravy and George, when he arrived, carved the turkeys.

We didn't leave the kitchen until well after ten o'clock that night, but it was a true Thanksgiving and one that we have never forgotten.

Friday November 28

You cannot teach a child to take care of himself unless you will let him try to take care of himself. He will make mistakes; and out of these mistakes will come his wisdom.

Henry Ward Beecher

Saturday November 29

My friend Muriel found this list on her husband's desk.

Chores to do before winter:
Clean the chimney
Chop and stack the firewood
Clean the furnace
Clean the storm windows.

Replace the weather stripping on all of the doors
Buy a snow blower
OR
Go south for the winter.

Sunday November 30

First Day in Advent

O come, O come, Emmanuel,
And ransom captive Israel,
That mourns in lowly exile here,
Until the son of God appear.
Rejoice! Rejoice! Emmanuel
Shall come to thee, O Israel

12th century Latin
Translated by Rev. J. M. Neale

December

Snow Picture

Yesterday hills and woods were gray,
And boughs were bare and brown
But all last night silently, silently
Snow came down.

All night long over the fields,
Quiet and soft and slow,
With never a footprint, steadily, steadily,
Walked the snow.

Now at dawn there is nothing but snow,
Nothing but whiteness now
Except the flame of a redbird's wing
On a feathery bough.

Never a sound in all the land;
Pure silence, through and through,
Save for the chatter of chickadees
Debating what to do.

Nancy Byrd Turner

Today brought the first significant snowfall, a prelude to winter, which arrives officially on the twenty first. The first snow is always exciting, and I'm happy to welcome our beautiful white world.

Tuesday December 2

Weather forecast: Snow—followed by little children on sleds.

Wednesday December 3

Judging from the number of people in the post office today, many of us had the same idea. We were mailing our out-of-town Christmas cards and parcels to friends and family who will not be with us during the holiday season.

I have been quite well organized this year and have managed to find many gifts at church craft sales. As well, Marg and I have made chili sauce, jam and fruit preserves that we enjoy giving to those friends who don't have the time to make their own. They seem to be very welcome gifts. As my husband George used to say, "You can never have too much homemade jam!"

Although we all spend much time finding thoughtful gifts to give, I believe these next lines best express the Christmas spirit.

Christmas is a time for giving,
The Wise Men brought their best,

But Christ showed the gift of self
Will out-give all the rest.

Thursday December 4

Life is the childhood of immortality.

Daniel A. Poling

Friday December 5

When the wind howls and blows snow around the doors and windows, it brings back memories of winters long years ago.

Back then, our home was heated with a coal furnace. I can still hear the sound coal made as it was emptied from the truck down the metal chute into the basement storage room. It started with a few tentative "clunks" that quickly became a roar as the coal dropped down to form a mountain on the basement floor.

And who can forget the many daily trips to the cellar to shovel scoopful after scoopful of coal into the furnace?

I confess that I enjoy turning up the thermostat and not having to shovel coal to warm up the house. People who talk about the "good old days" must have very short memories.

Saturday December 6

Will and Muriel stopped by for tea today. They had just come from a visit with an elderly friend who is living in a nursing home. At

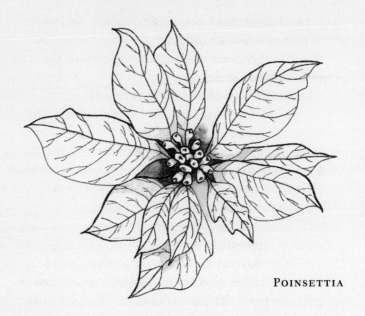

POINSETTIA

this time of year when we are caught up in decorating, shopping and entertaining, we sometimes neglect those who can't easily get out. Christmas is often the time when we are most needed, because it can be a very lonely season for those who have few friends or relatives still living.

Make someone else's day a little happier and you are sure to have brightened your own.

Sunday December 7

When I was growing up on Canada's east coast, the weather during Advent was often considered to be a harbinger of the winter to come. It was an old Acadian belief that a cold, miserable Advent meant that we would have a mild winter. If Advent was more temperate, it was almost sure to be a long and harsh winter.

The Advent season has its own special traditions. The Advent wreath, the circle of greenery in which four candles are set, originated with the German Lutherans. The Advent calendar also originated in Germany. The most popular of the calendars have a piece of chocolate for each day as a treat for the youngsters who are anxiously awaiting the arrival of Christmas.

In the past, Advent was a period of fasting when no meat, cheese or alcoholic drinks could be consumed. This is no longer true, although some do choose to fast at this time.

Rev. W. B. Collyer wrote one of the most well known Advent hymns.

Great God, what do I see and hear?
The end of things created:
The judge of all men doth appear
On clouds of glory seated:
The trumpet sounds, the graves restore
The dead which they contained before;
Prepare, my soul, to meet Him.

Monday December 8

We get the sweetest comfort
When we wear the oldest shoe.
We love the old friends better
Than we'll ever love the new.

Old friends are more appealing
To the wearied heart—and so
We find the best enjoyment
With friends of long ago.

There's a kind of mellow sweetness
In a good thing growing old.
Each year that rolls around it
Leaves an added touch of gold.

Author unknown

How wonderful it is to receive Christmas cards from old friends! In some cases this may be our only contact in the year, but with such friends it's as if I can hear them say, "So, as I was saying . . ."

Tuesday December 9

Kay and Ken Rogers, good friends and neighbours, had a wonderful party this evening. Since 1988 they have invited all of the neighbours to this soiree. It's special because each person attending must bring a donation: a toy, a game or food, to be distributed to needy families.

Once again this party was an enormous success. People enjoyed themselves immensely, and the Rogers collected hundreds of dollars worth of nourishing food, and toys that will delight many youngsters on Christmas morning.

Thanks to the Rogers' kindness, it will be a merrier Christmas for many.

Wednesday December 10

Now is the season of the holly and mistletoe; the days are come in which we hang our rooms with the sober green of December and feel it summer in our hearts.

Saturday Evening Post
December 29, 1866

Thursday December 11

The Jewish celebration of Hanukkah, also known as the festival of lights, commemorates the miracle that happened during the rededication of the Hebrew temple in Israel in 165 B.C. At that time, a one-day supply of oil to cleanse the temple burned for a miraculous eight days. That long-burning flame is remembered with the lighting of the candles on the menorah every sunset for eight days.

I wish a Happy Hanukkah and the special joy of family times together for all of my Jewish friends.

Friday December 12

It has the shine of tinsel,
Of crisp and frosty ground,
The very name of Christmas,
Has sparkle in its sound.

Saturday December 13

At this time of year many parents are looking for a project that will keep small children included in the holiday preparations. A snowglobe to keep or give to someone special is sure to delight youngsters and make a cherished keepsake for friends or family members.

You will need:
—jars
—figurines
—oil based paint
—paintbrush
—sandpaper
—superglue
—water
—glitter
—glycerin

Almost any kind of jar will do; baby food or spaghetti sauce jars are good choices. Avoid tall skinny jars because they won't accommodate a figurine; as well, jars with writing on them may take away from the look of the finished product. Be sure that the lids are a tight fit and don't leak. Clean and dry the jars thoroughly.

Plastic or ceramic figurines can be found in craft stores or cake decorating shops. Choose figurines that are a good fit for the jars you have.

Paint the outside of the jar lids with an oil-based paint in your favorite colour. Sand the inside of the lid until it is no longer smooth. Glue the figurine to the inside of the lid and allow to dry.

Fill the jar with water almost to the top. Sprinkle a pinch of glitter in the water and add a touch of glycerin. This keeps the glitter from falling too quickly. Do not add too much glycerin because it will stick to the bottom of the jar. Screw the lid on tightly. Turn the jar over and back again to let it snow.

Sunday December 14

How I love the hymns of the season! We sang one of my particular favourites in church this morning.

Once in royal David's city,
Stood a lowly cattle shed,
Where a mother laid her baby
In a manger for his bed;
Mary was that mother mild,
Jesus Christ her little child.

Cecil Frances Alexander

Monday December 15

Christmas is anticipation and discovery, dazzling lights and brilliant colours. Christmas is the gentle smile of someone dear, the quiet, heartwarming traditions. Christmas is home and family and love.

Barbara Burrow

Tuesday December 16

The people of Mexico have a most interesting way to prepare for Christmas. A nine-day celebration, from December 16 to 24, commemorates the journey of Mary and Joseph from Nazareth to Bethlehem and their search for shelter. The processions, or *losadas*, take place each night for nine nights as a couple, dressed as Joseph and Mary, go from home to home seeking shelter. As it was in Bethlehem, the couple are turned away until they knock on the door of the home that has been chosen to host the party that evening. With their arrival, the *posada* (party) begins. The highlight of each party is the breaking of the piñata. The children are blindfolded and given a chance to swing a stick at the piñata, a papier mâché animal hanging by a string from the ceiling and filled with toys and candies.

The *posadas* are repeated for nine evenings, the last being Christmas Eve. On that evening, known as *Noche Bueno* or the Good Night, the pilgrimage ends when the procession arrives at the church for midnight Mass. This Mass is known as the *Misa de Gallo*, or Mass of the Rooster, because it is held so early.

Good friends of mine, Jim and Betty Lucas, lived for many years in Mexico City. They told me of this interesting ritual that they remember fondly. It is always nice to learn the traditions of other countries and know that we are celebrating the birth of the Messiah in our own ways.

Wednesday December 17

One hundred years ago today, Orville and Wilbur Wright brought to reality the centuries-old dream of soaring with the eagles. Their short flight at Kitty Hawk, North Carolina, was the beginning of the advances that allowed men to walk on the moon.

Thursday December 18

"People often warn us against letting the golden hours slip by; but some of them are golden only because we let them slip by."

These words came to mind today as I sat by the fire and read a book. My Christmas cards are sent, the presents are wrapped, the baking is done and preparations for the big day are complete. This afternoon I decided that I needed some time just for me; so I lit a fire, pulled out a good book, and the hours simply vanished. I truly appreciate this "golden" time.

WHITE CHRISTMAS

Friday December 19

I watched a number of youngsters sledding on the hill in our park today. One child, shouting happily, was on his brand new, brightly coloured coaster. His friend, equally happy, was sliding down the hill on the cardboard box that the sled came in.

Saturday December 20

Jamie and Marshall hosted a Christmas party at their home this evening. It was a large group and rather noisy, and my great-grandson Michael was heard to remark, "Wow, this is fun . . . it's like being in our school lunchroom."

Sunday December 21

The people that walked in darkness have seen a great light: they that dwell in the land of the shadow of death, upon them hath the light shined.

For unto us a child is born, unto us a son is given: and the government shall be upon his shoulder: and his name shall be called Wonderful, Counsellor, The mighty God, The everlasting Father, The Prince of Peace.

Isaiah 9:2, 6

Monday December 22

At Christmas time, there are the things I know:

Fragrance of pine, air frosted, keen with
  snow;
Laughter of children, raised in glad surprise;
Breathless expectancy; the smiling eyes
Of friends with gifts white-clad and ribbon
  tied;
Odor of good things cooking. There abide
The dearest things I know in all the earth:
Home and loved ones, friendship, song and
  mirth.

Author unknown

Tuesday December 23

Winter has come and the trees are now bare,
You feel all her wrath on the cold frosty air.

Wednesday December 24

Our family's custom is to enjoy a light supper, usually soup and a sandwich, before heading off to church to watch the children's presentation of the Christmas story. Marg made a delicious cream of carrot and cheddar cheese soup to serve this evening. The recipe will serve 4, but is easily doubled for a larger group.

Cream of Carrot and Cheddar Cheese Soup

1 tbsp. vegetable oil
1 onion, chopped
6 carrots, chopped

5 cups chicken stock (or chicken broth)
2 tbsp. rice
1 tsp. Worcestershire sauce
1/4 tsp. dried thyme
1 tbsp. parsley flakes
1 bay leaf
dash of hot pepper sauce
pinch of pepper (salt optional)
1 1/2 cups 2% milk
1 cup old cheddar cheese, shredded

In a large saucepan, heat oil over medium heat; add onion and cook for 5 minutes, stirring occasionally. Add carrots, chicken stock, rice, Worcestershire sauce, thyme, parsley flakes, bay leaf, hot pepper sauce, pepper; bring to a boil. Reduce heat to low and simmer 25 minutes or until carrots are tender. Discard bay leaf. In a blender, puree the soup in batches; return to pan. Stir in milk. Bring to simmer; stir in cheddar cheese and cook over low heat until melted. Add salt to taste.

Thursday December 25

Christmas is such a joyful time in the Christian life. It is a time of twinkling stars at midnight and soft prayers whispered in the candlelight. It is a time of carolling and bells jingling in the frosty air. It is a time of holly and bows and tinsel and gifts. Christmas is a time to remember our friends far and near and a time to remember the child in a manger so very long ago.

Merry Christmas!

Friday December 26

Angels from the realms of glory,
Wing your flight o'er all the earth;
Ye who sang creation's story,
Now proclaim Messiah's birth:
Come and worship,
Worship Christ, the new-born King.

James Montgomery
Book of Common Prayer

Saturday December 27

Henry Van Dyke made this observation on Christmas gifts: "If every gift is the token of a personal thought, a friendly feeling, an unselfish interest in the joys of others, then the thought, the feeling, the interest may remain long after the gift is forgotten."

Sunday December 28

Almighty God, who desirest not the death of sinners but rather that they may turn unto Thee and love, deliver the nations of the world from superstition and unbelief. Gather them into Thy Holy Church, to the praise and glory of Thy name, through Jesus Christ our Lord. Amen.

Book of Common Prayer

Monday December 29

The morning mail brought a delightful surprise.

For the last several years I had lost touch with an old friend from my childhood. We grew up together on Canada's east coast, married around the same time and had our families . . . me with my three girls, and Laura with her three boys. Although we didn't live close to each other as our children grew up, we maintained contact through letters and phone calls, sharing our joys and sorrows as only old friends can.

About three years ago my Christmas card was returned with a "not at this address" notation. A phone call produced "This number is no longer in service." I was devastated.

You can imagine my surprise then, as I opened the card, to see Laura's familiar handwriting, albeit a little more shaky. She wrote, "Edna, I hope this letter finds you well. You must wonder where I've been. Well, I suffered a severe stroke and I have been in the hospital and rehabilitation centres for these many long months. I couldn't talk, walk or communicate. At first I wanted to die, but my sons and daughters-in-law, my grandchildren and great-grandchildren would not let that happen. They had me moved to a hospital closer to them and set about helping me to get well. Their love and patience along with the help of the doctors, nurses and therapists has finally allowed me to find "me" again.

"I have missed our friendship and hope to hear from you very soon."

We sometimes receive a gift whose value cannot be measured. This is such a gift!

Tuesday December 30

The closing hours approach of the old year.
His aged head is white, his face is sere.
Though cheerful yet, and will be to the last:
O may the years as peacefully be passed
That age may find thee still with smiling eyes
That look with joy expectant to the skies.

Author unknown

Wednesday December 31

New Year's Eve—how quickly the days and months seem to have passed this year.

I am thankful for the many blessings and achievements of the year gone by and look forward to the new year with faith and hope and the belief that the best is yet to come.

May this new year bring you all good health and much happiness!